The Making of an Angler

The Making of an Angler

by Bob Elliot

with solemn, genteel and dignified illustrations by Dink Siegel

WINCHESTER PRESS

ACKNOWLEDGMENTS

I owe something to everybody with whom I have gone fishing, read about fishing and dreamed about fishing. Three individuals should be given particular credit, my agent Lurton Blassingame, editor Robert Elman and artist Dink Siegel.

Library of Congress Catalog Card Number: 74–16865
ISBN: 0–87691–160–2

Published by Winchester Press
205 East 42nd Street, New York 10017

PRINTED IN THE UNITED STATES OF AMERICA

to

gamefishes and guides
who opened their mouths
for my barbs.

Contents

Foreword

Unless one is engaged in commercial fishing, it seems to me that angling should be fun. Maybe that strikes you as too obvious to need saying, yet I'll wager you can remember fishing sessions or even days or whole seasons when the fun—the whole reason for being on the water—was smothered in the frustrated determination to outwit the quarry or master some elusive skill. I sometimes wonder if, in our attempts to match hatches precisely and to ennoble finned quarries, we may not be missing casts for human friendships and catches of uninhibited laughter.

The true Downeast Mainer still places value on his sense of humor—perhaps because his ancestors found life so hard and nature so challenging that they learned to survive by telling one another, "Might as well laugh as cry." Or, as my grandmother often reminded me when my juvenile tears fell, "Go on and bawl! The more you cry, the less you'll urinate."

I have written serious fishing books and sections in others which should suffice to impress my peers—at least those in my own family—so, this one is going to be different.

Readers are warned now that I will be laughing at myself (and perhaps at some of them) as I relate some of the things that have happened along the piscatorial way in The Making of an Angler.

Publishers are convinced (probably with complete justification) that readers seldom recall an outdoor writer from one book to the next. Often, therefore, an author is asked to present his "credentials" in a foreword, thus persuading readers that he is qualified to pontificate on his chosen subject. Very well, then, I will here reveal a little of my background in the hope that, by some mystical process, it will convince the world that I have caught fish on something besides (not to the exclusion of but in addition to) a worm-baited handline.

Early in life I bragged that my mother once told me her side of the family was descended from English nobility, and a Maine farm boy said I needn't worry about that, that he wouldn't hold it against me so long as I tried hard to live it down. With this riposte in mind ever afterward, I gradually invented an ancestry that was more to my own liking, even if my living relatives wanted me speechless.

For example:

Somebody once asked me about my high cheekbones and I told him: "A maternal ancestor was taken prisoner during King Philip's War in Colonial times. Since she preferred rape to a scalping, I inherited my aquiline features."

We had five generations in the family on my mother's side when I was one of what the books now call the little people. So I heard many conversations about happenings in the clan. A half sister of mine was older than one of her aunts, since my grandmother and my mother, widowed at the same time, remarried and bore offspring in the foregoing order. (That made my half-sister's aunt only a half-aunt, too.)

There was so much talk about honor and virtue on the part

of the feminine gender in that period that I later began to wonder how any family was perpetuated. The solution struck my devious mind when I was studying transitive and intransitive verbs. "If one lies down, one may get laid." I decided. But back to my ancestry. Somebody once asked me a more personal question and I guess this one got to me, for I snapped:

"Well, my paternal ancestors were Scots and my father told me we were descended from Robin Hood's Merrie Men—specifically from Little Jock the Robber."

It was with this kind of background and this sort of mind that I became reconciled early in life to my own limitations and decided that, since my chances of becoming President were limited, I might as well relax and go fishing. At every opportunity. With the smallest excuse to my parents—and later to my wife and family—I did so.

Not that my mother didn't try to make me into a worthy citizen. She reminded me daily that a man can do anything he sets his mind on accomplishing. "Nothing is impossible!" she reiterated.

But there was this person whom I idolized from the time I could walk and on all through his fourscore years and ten. He was my grandmother's third husband; after going through two others, she apparently had decided to wed a younger man, for he was a year or two the junior of my mother, even if he was her step-stepfather.

As a boy, I went fishing with him in a sailing sloop. Once when we were handlining off the Maine coast, I mentioned my lack of initiative.

"Your mother's *mostly* right," he agreed. "You can be about anything you set your mind to, given a few brains. But," he went on, with a smile, "that part about *nothing* being impossible—that makes me wonder a bit. Like, for instance, do you think a man could stand on his head and crap in his shirt pocket?"

"See what you mean," I admitted.

Yet I had to go to work sooner or later and, after spending one winter as a carpenter's apprentice with my father, I thought I never would have warm hands and feet again, regardless of how long I might live. In desperation, I went to work for a small-town weekly newspaper and learned the business by setting type, making up forms, running the press and helping to fold the papers for distribution.

Within a year or two, the owner won election to the state legislature and I was left to write copy for both news and advertising columns.

At every opportunity I went fishing: mornings from daylight to starting time on the paper; evenings from quitting time until dark; weekends, if I could steal the time. Still single, after four years of this, I returned to school, studying journalism in Boston and working odd hours on a daily paper in that city.

Perhaps it was then that I first heard about publicity. Later on, when promoters decided to elevate themselves to vice-presidents instead of remaining "tub-thumpers," the term "Public Relations" impressed me.

(I have come to believe in later life that, despite the prestige and high salaries usually associated with public-relations positions, there are many in this field who are unqualified. They seem to think "Public Relations" means having relations in public.)

Nevertheless, in due time I started working at this activity, first for a New England state fish and game department, part-time, then for the State of Maine, where I was originally employed to encourage the sale of fishing and hunting licenses and the occupancy of sporting camps as well as to improve economic conditions generally by writing about and photographing outdoor participant sports. (If I can claim no other earthshaking success, I can state unequivocally that I was not the sort of outdoor public-relations man who confuses sporting camps with sporting houses.)

Now, if I were to become authoritative about my subjects, I must participate in them officially, fishing and hunting no longer purely for fun but for business.

Imagine a clergyman learning religion in Paradise; a musician attuned permanently to heavenly chords; an artist whose vision reached beyond the spectrum—and you can picture my life during the next quarter of a century.

Not only could I search out hidden trout and salmon waters, lying like rare, shining jewels within Maine's 17 million acres of woodlands, but I must follow her seacoast and seek striped bass, tuna, pollock and mackerel. I must make friends of woods and water guides, of game wardens, wildlife and fisheries biologists, fishing- and hunting-lodge managers, sportsmen, outdoor writers, photographers, local and national public officials.

Sometimes it was difficult to find time to cast a fly or pull a trigger, for there were conventions and conferences in many parts of the United States and Canada with increasing regularity as time went on. (Of course, there were free days when I might fish or hunt during some of the conventions. So it wasn't a total loss.)

As other participant sports grew in popularity, my work included promotion of these to encourage tourism on a wider basis and to spread vacationers' interests widely enough to relieve pressures on wildlife resources. Today it would take more than two Maine trout to feed a multitude; indeed, a miracle would need to be re-enacted to satisfy the hunger of five thousand people, if salmon were cooked and divided amongst them. But in the ocean there still are bluefin tuna of 600 and 700 pounds, of course. Thus, I might have called this book "Two Fishes," leaving out the word "Small," but, regardless of length or weight, I still find the Eastern brook trout my preference, and the 2-ounce rod and dry fly remain my favorite tools.

If I never hooked and released another brookie, though, I could live on the memories of the literally thousands of fishing trips I have made. I wonder sometimes if I have perhaps enjoyed the friendship of all those I have met while fishing and hunting fully as much as I have been thrilled by the excitement of the chase.

And maybe, after all, my mother was right when she insisted a man might become the kind of person he wished to be and that he might accomplish whatever he set his mind to achieving. If the trout are there and I am allotted time enough, I can get them to strike. I can play them to within reach, release them carefully, and take them again another day.

Worthier goals than these certainly should have been sought and they still lie there in my past, waiting to be picked up by anybody who has ambition, courage, daring, persistence and faith in himself without limit. I will them to the first man who claims them.

I hope you don't follow my example and not amount to much as a result but, if you are interested in some of the experiences that made me what I am today, you will find them and the people whose lives have touched mine in the chapters that follow. Some of my reminiscences will perhaps make a point or two about fishing. Others may have little direct connection and yet I hope they will make a larger point—that some of the best stories are told by fishing friends and guides; the joke-swapping, the pranks, the tall tales, the ramblings, the camaraderie—all those elements of the outdoor experience may not teach anyone the difference between a tippet and a tip-up but they are vital to the making of an angler and they add immeasurably to the fun of fishing.

BOB ELLIOT
Augusta, Maine
Forty-Eight Hours and Several Minutes Before
Opening Day, 1974

1

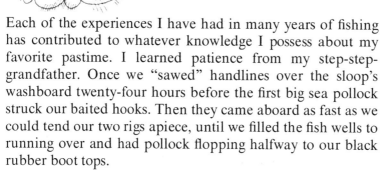

FIRST QUALIFICATION:

Patience

Each of the experiences I have had in many years of fishing has contributed to whatever knowledge I possess about my favorite pastime. I learned patience from my step-step-grandfather. Once we "sawed" handlines over the sloop's washboard twenty-four hours before the first big sea pollock struck our baited hooks. Then they came aboard as fast as we could tend our two rigs apiece, until we filled the fish wells to running over and had pollock flopping halfway to our black rubber boot tops.

When we put into Kennebunkport to sell our haul, one discouraged fisherman, who had quit the shoals long before we came put-putting in on the old auxiliary make-and-break engine, shouted: "I got ne'er a pollock. Did you get e'er a pollock?" And the old man said: "Ayah. Picked up a few hundredweight."

I remembered this when I lived on the New Hampshire seacoast, where I had faced a standoff from striped bass for several weekends in a row. At low tide in a river I often fished, I had seen schools of six- and eight-pound stripers nosing mussels from the channel mud, in water so shallow their backs stuck out as they worked. So I well knew they were there; it was simply a question of catching them.

To make things a little more challenging, I persisted in trying to take them on streamer flies. As the tide neared low-water, I cast until my arm ached. I never got a touch.

After lunch on the final Saturday afternoon I fished for this particular school of stripers, I launched my small skiff and drifted downstream a couple of miles, casting and trolling a blue and white bucktail on two five-ounce fly rods. Then I worked the shallow channel at full ebb tide and, as the flow turned inward, I followed it back upriver. Darkness descended. I ate a sandwich, drank some coffee and continued casting and trolling flies.

Weary, sleepy and disillusioned, worried about what my family would think, I dozed at intervals in the skiff.

It was high tide about 11 o'clock that evening. I decided I had better quit and go home. As I made a final, despairing cast, a bass smashed the fly savagely and tore off line down to the backing. I got the striper turned, finally, so it had to fight the tide as well as the pressure from my rod and I brought it alongside and boated a fish I found later weighed eight pounds. Meanwhile, the rod in the rod holder was bowed, the reel singing. I seized it and after a time boated a second bass of similar size.

For two hours I fought bass as fast as I could cast and bring them alongside. On light tackle, this meant about a dozen stripers, all told, for it took at least 10 minutes on each fish.

Now I absolutely had to go home and let my family know I still lived! Used to my errant ways, they weren't so concerned as might have been expected and the catch of fish— for it was the time of the Great Depression—compensated partially for my absence.

Graduated—as obnoxious as this word is, I know, to a salt-water sportsman—from tidal fishing to the so-called "fine art" of casting No. 18 dry fluffs on two-ounce rods for the noble Eastern brook trout these many years since that day, I still find patience and persistence to be not only twin virtues but essential human qualities for trouting success.

As recently as mid-June of this year, I chanced to fish for brook trout in the one- to two-pound class, while visiting a remote pond in Maine's southern Aroostook County. Another writer and I had been driven there in an ingenious device, designed and built for crawling uphill over otherwise impassable roads, even for a four-wheel-drive vehicle. This rig had caterpillar treads and on each side, over the treads, were platforms wide enough to stand on. A pipe railing was attached at hand-high position. Our fishing gear was hauled behind in a homemade trailer.

After driving in a truck as far as we could that day, we journeyed the remaining two or three miles on this unit and, when we took as much arm-wracking and jolting as we could stand, we would hop off and hike the hill for a few minutes before boarding it again.

Eventually we arrived at a place where we had to walk along a woodland trail for perhaps another half-mile. All at once the pond was in view and our pulses beat faster. It had to be full of trout! A place this difficult to reach just had to be brimming over with wild brookies.

Two aluminum canoes came from their hiding spots and we were ferried over to a tiny log cabin, where we left the nonessentials, set up our rods and said we were ready to go fishing.

A good friend of ours operates a fishing lodge in northern Maine and he maintains outlying camps like the one on the tiny pond we were visiting. He had given me several small streamer flies that were "sure to take trout every cast."

They didn't that afternoon. We fished them completely around the shoreline, crossed and crisscrossed the water without getting so much as a touch.

Then, each of us switched to dependable patterns like

Black Ghost, Gray Ghost, Red and White Bucktail, Mickey Finn . . . all to no avail.

We fished nymphs, wet flies and cast dries. Nothing doing.

Finally, since we had to leave well before dark, my companion writer went back to the cabin and began taking pictures from that vantage point. I kept casting, using all dry flies now, since if I'm not catching trout anyhow I prefer to not catch them on dries.

The sun set and our cameraman called us nearer to the cabin, taking silhouettes of my casting, with trees, sky, canoe, and the guide and me reflected in the smooth pond surface. He was rapturous over the scene. But I was still determined to catch a trout or two in the few minutes left before we must start back out.

A white moth fluttered across the canoe bow and fell on the surface. There was a slight break in the water beneath the struggling wings and the moth disappeared. I told my guide: "Hold the canoe right here, please."

Quickly, I exchanged a Brown Wulff which I had been casting for a White Wulff, size 8. I sprayed it with a flotant and cast it toward the spot where the trout had fed a moment or two previously.

The fly lay unnoticed momentarily and I began to retrieve it toward the canoe in short hops, with idle resting periods between twitches of the rod. As it floated, now, within a few feet of the canoe, I started to lift the rod and fly for another cast. A trout followed it and when I saw the break I struck and felt his weight for a fraction of a second. Then he was gone.

I dried the White Wulff and watched the surface of the pond for feeding trout. Now I spotted a fluttering moth on the water an easy cast away and immediately I dropped my artificial beside the dying insect. When I worked the rod, so the Wulff danced lightly, a brookie came up and out and took the fly going down in a wild, savage way that caused us to cry out simultaneously.

"That's more like it!" said the guide.

When we finally maneuvered the trout to net I decided to

keep it for pictures. It was a fat, colorful fish, darker than those that ordinarily live in mountain streams. Indeed, this pond trout was blackish-green in places and its belly was nearer red than orange. We checked and found that it weighed a pound and a half.

Once more I dropped the white fly into a circle that indicated a feeding trout and soon we had another fish of similar size in the net.

Now trout began to come up all over the pond. But we had to heed our companion's call, warning us it would be dark before we got out of the woods if we didn't hurry.

As we came to the dock I glanced at my watch. I had been casting for more than five hours! Yet I had been totally absorbed all the while, not once thinking of those many problems we all face in life but considering only how to outwit those brookies all of that afternoon and early evening; knowing that, with patience, I should do so eventually.

"Tomorrow morning at sunrise might be a time of fast action," I thought. "But we won't be here then."

On the long ride back in the truck from where we left the caterpillar-tread vehicle, my companions remarked on the way I had stayed with my casting. I told them I lose sense of time and forget responsibilities when I'm fishing. They nodded in agreement.

"Once I wrote a short story on that theme," I said. "I wove a thread of sex interest into the yarn, but, while one editor wrote he thought it had some earthy humor, his staff decided it didn't play up the sex angle strongly enough. I tossed it in a drawer and went back to writing purely fishing and hunting articles."

"What was the yarn about?" a guide asked.

That was all the encouragement I needed. As we lurched and bounced over the logging roads back to our base lodge, I related the story to them. It went like this . . .

2

EXPERIMENTATION, OR

The Honeymoon Bucktail

Ol' Foamy, as he was known in college, acquired his nickname as somewhat of a champion among champion beer drinkers. His father, consumed by fishing fever, knelt often at the altar of Izaak Walton, and he had intended to name his only son after that star in the constellation Pisces, which supposedly resembles a fish in shape. However, the old man, being weak on astronomy, confused Pisces with the more southerly constellation Piscis Austrinus and thus had his offspring christened Fomalhaut, for one of the stars in the wrong constellation. A beer drinker of his magnitude and with that name was bound to be called Ol' Foamy by his fraternity brothers.

Ol' Foamy never set his dad right. He was an emotional son and his fondness for fishing exceeded even that of his parent (though some people found this hard to believe, since

6

Ol' Foamy spent so much time making love to an endless number of beautiful girls that they didn't see how he had time left to check his flies, let alone cast delicate artificials).

Still unwed at thirty years of age, Ol' Foamy had, until comparatively recent months, been content to fish all spring, summer and fall, tie flies all winter and do what else came naturally in his spare time from fishing.

Friends gave him a birthday party when he turned thirty. Looking at his strong, masculine, well-tanned face and magnificent body, mothers of eligible daughters kept reminding him of his duty to society. His father, still going strong and without other heirs to his considerable fortune, urged Ol' Foamy to choose a beauty from his stable of *femmes fatales* and sire an offspring who could, in time, matriculate into their alma mater, join the right fraternity and, above all, carry on their heritage of fishing with an ethical, English-tied strictly dry fly.

Eventually the pressures got to Ol' Foamy. He went to a psychoanalyst (a man he knew liked to fish) and admitted that, as much as he loved to love and be loved, he had on certain occasions lately passed up passionate pad-mates for dates with brook trout or salmon in far-off places.

His analyst told Ol' Foamy the answer was obvious: Marry a girl who would rather fish than fraternize but who would not be averse to either delightful activity.

The word got around that Ol' Foamy might consider wedlock and he soon was besieged by double-tapered *femes sole,* kittens readily recognized as sex symbols, models, even mature divorcées with experience at leading young rams to the altar.

Still, as he confessed to his analyst, every time he went fishing he became so absorbed in the sport that girl business was washed out of his mind. His fishing doctor looked at him so sadly Ol' Foamy worried even more.

One day he entered his favorite New York tackle shop. Automatically, he stepped aside at the elevator to allow a girl to go in first and as he followed he noticed they were the only occupants.

Ol' Foamy was intrigued by her exotic perfume. His initial glance became a fixed stare. She was unbelievably beautiful—gorgeous, magnificent! His scrutiny took in her crown of jet-black hair, her paper-white classical features and the faint flush his appraisement caused.

Her neck was well molded, and her body! From that ivory column down to her toes, she surpassed anything even such a a practiced connoisseur as Ol' Foamy had dreamed of, let alone viewed.

He thought: "Lord, it's a wonder she doesn't burst right out of that sheath dress. What a vision if she should!"

She left the elevator on the third floor and he followed her in a daze. As she slithered ahead in a corridor between counters, he saw that her hips not only rotated but moved forward and back in a series of near bumps and grinds.

When she halted, apparently waiting for him to catch up, he was so flustered he stood there swinging one foot back and forth and blushing like a schoolboy.

"I'm looking for an appropriate fishing book for a friend," she murmured, throatily. "You look like an angler. Perhaps you can advise me. Should I get one on wet-fly fishing, do you think, or would a book on dry flies be more fitting?"

He said, "Well . . ."

"Perhaps you'd help me select one," she continued.

They went along to the book section. When the sales manager saw Ol' Foamy he came rushing up.

"Personal attention for good customers like you, Mr. Smith," he began. Then his eyes popped. He stared at Ol' Foamy with open envy and kept moistening his lips, as if they were chapped.

("Now you tell us!" interposed one of the guides in the truck we were still riding back to camp.

("Tell you what?" I asked, still wrapped in my storytelling and not wanting to lose its thread.

("That the guy's name was Smith. Wasn't one of your ancestors a Smith?"

("Yeah, sure. My great grandfather from Cape Cod who sailed into Kennebunkport as a boy and married the girl who was to become my great grandmother. The old gentleman was named Benjamin Rhoades Smith and he once told me that Granny and he were married sixty-seven years and that they never let the sun go down on their wrath."

("Figgered if they was goin' to fight, it sure as hell wasn't going to be in bed," the guide remarked. "Them old-timers warn't so dumb."

("My God," I expostulated, "what's that got to do with the yarn I'm trying to tell you?"

("He just likes to keep things neat and tied up the way they should be," my outdoor-writer companion said.

("Go on with your story. We won't interrupt again. Provided," he told the other guide, "you pass me a can of beer from that cooler."

("Fishermen!" I exclaimed. "We're all a bit peculiar, but the ones I pick for friends beat 'em all."

(They urged me to continue my yarn.)

Ol' Foamy selected a few fishing books from the better-known titles on the shelves in that New York store where they had met. He told the salesman not to bother.

"We'll just browse a bit."

He steered the beautiful girl to a secluded corner and found a bench for them to sit on. She snuggled close and as they inadvertently brushed arms and legs, Ol' Foamy experienced a series of shocks the like of which he hadn't felt since adolescence.

"Now, Miss . . .?"

"Dusky Jones. Not a nickname; my hair has always been inky black and my parents thought Dusky fitted me best."

"It does, it does," he agreed, rapturously. "Jones and Smith; Smith and Jones; Dusky, Foamy . . ."

"Do you feel okay?"

She touched his arm softly and looked at him with warm eyes that were as blue as her hair was black. They were enigmatic eyes, he thought.

"Lord! I've really been hit by this one. This is it! This solves my problem. I've got it made.

"Do you like to fish?"

"Love to," she told him.

With the direct tactics that had made him so successful a Casanova in the past, he told her now:

"I'll put half a dozen of these books on my own account. Then we'll go to my place and I'll fill you in on their contents, so you can make a wise decision."

She demurred that they hardly knew each other but he assured her they would soon leap that hurdle.

"One book really is enough. How about this?"

She read the title: *"Fishing with a Nymph."*

Ol' Foamy trembled, but he had played too many trout to rush things and he answered: "We'll take the lot."

None of his friends and least of all Ol' Foamy himself would believe that he could act as precipitously as he did in the next five days. He bought her a gigantic diamond that same afternoon, filed for a marriage license, purchased plane tickets to Montreal, and reserved a bush pilot to fly them into a remote wilderness lake in northern Quebec Province where, a friend assured him, "Speckled trout weigh four and five pounds—if you can catch them!"

He was told they could use a private camp—the only one on the lake—for their honeymoon.

Dusky never mentioned *her* fishing acquaintance again, and the books they had purchased went on a shelf in Ol' Foamy's apartment, along with many others.

She was radiant. Ol' Foamy absorbed her time and she had to shop for her wedding by telephone. He held her in his arms as though he thought she might disappear. She responded in a way that consumed him but she withheld the final peak of their passion for their wedding night.

He was frustrated, feverish with longing. Her eyes shone with desire to match his own when, in response to her question, "Will you pack your own fishing tackle, or shall I?" he replied:

"We'll leave it here. You'll be my greatest catch, Dusky, darling!"

Their wedding was a memorable event. Men swore over his luck; countless girls cried regretfully. But they broke away prematurely from the reception to catch their plane and soon found themselves in Canada. Romantic French Customs officers shooed them along and soon they were in the float plane, en route to the wilderness trout lake.

Ol' Foamy came to with a start when the pilot sideslipped down and taxied to a dock just below a log cabin. While the pilot toted their luggage, Ol' Foamy carried his bride across the threshold.

A caretaker had started a fire. It blazed in the open fireplace. Hors d'oeuvres and liquors were spread for them and a note explained that a buffet was ready in the dining room at their pleasure.

They had a quick drink, nibbled a few canapés and then Dusky kissed Ol' Foamy long and passionately.

"I'm going upstairs and shower," she whispered. "I'll find our room and be ready in a few minutes."

Ol' Foamy took up their bags. As she disappeared into the shower, he gave her another searing kiss and then trotted off downstairs, already, he thought, like an obedient husband.

As he explored the lodge, he noted a glass case in one corner of a small den.

"Hmm!" His friend certainly had a fine assortment of fly rods. Ol' Foamy eyed them with growing appreciation. He took out one at a time and whipped them carefully.

"Sweet action! Beautiful!"

Just for kicks, why not stroll down to the dock and make a few casts. She wouldn't be showered for a while.

The rods were all rigged with reels, lines and leaders and there were books of flies handy.

As Ol' Foamy stepped onto the dock a huge brook trout broke completely out of water and arced back in with a tremendous splash. Feverishly, Ol' Foamy worked out line and then dropped a big dry Wulff on the surface.

"That trout must weigh six pounds!" he breathed.

Yet he didn't get a strike.

There was a canoe on the dock and Ol' Foamy launched it. Picking up a paddle, he stroked the canoe slowly along, making casts in likely-looking spots. Every few minutes, a huge brookie would come clear out of water, as the one had at the dock, but nothing he offered brought a hit.

Time was lost. The sun set. Then the pond really came alive. Some sort of insect was hatching and flying upward, mating, then dropping back to be gobbled by trout after trout. Ol' Foamy picked one from the lake and saw that it was a bluish-black. He tried a Black Wulff. Nothing doing.

Finally, he paddled back to the dock. As he climbed from the canoe and walked dazedly up the path to the lodge, he realized with a jolt that he had muffed a momentous occasion.

"My God! What will she think of me?"

He sneaked into the cabin like a chastened schoolboy, removed his moccasins and tiptoed to their room. A small night light glowed. Ol' Foamy felt like an intruder.

It was warm in the room. Sweet, lovely, gorgeous, desirable Dusky lay quite nude on the nuptial bed. One arm cradled her jet-black hair. She breathed quietly and the fall and rise of her breasts gave life to what otherwise might have seemed a Greek goddess.

Ol' Foamy studied his bride. Fine blue-black hair curled in her armpits and in a deep valley below. Against her chaste white flesh, the hair was striking.

Suddenly he knew what was bothering him. "Why, that body hair is identical in coloration to the mayflies those big trout are taking!"

Dusky's manicure kit was on a nearby table. Ol' Foamy crept to it, pulled out a pair of scissors and, with surgeon-like care lest she awaken, he cut a few strands of pubic hair from her body.

Sneaking downstairs, he soon found a fly-tying kit and assembled a couple of big dry Wulffs.

This time a five-pound trout smashed the fly on Ol' Foamy's first cast from the dock. He hadn't stopped for any spray to dry the flies, so he changed to his other untried Dusky and took another, even heavier fish on his second cast.

He trotted back to the lodge, dragging those two lunkers behind him. As he stepped inside he heard a light humming noise. Logs blazed brazenly in the fireplace and there, standing with one foot on a hassock, was the still nude Dusky, busily running an electric razor.

As the very last of the pubic hair fell to the floor, Dusky glanced up at her stupefied swain.

"Obviously the trout love me, anyhow," she said.

"We both do! That is, I do, too!"

She glided up beside him. He dropped the trout. Passion throbbed in her throaty voice and her vibrant flesh quivered. He was filled with certain misgivings but also with ardent desire. She placed her arms around him.

"Wash off that fishy smell," she ordered. "Now, listen to me. Every man is entitled to one last fling, I know. But, Brother, you've just had yours. From now on, *my* hobby comes first."

(The truck rumbled into the yard beside our own fishing camp. One of the guides sighed.

("Tell me something. Did that girl really like to fish, too?"

(I laughed. "Your fantasy is of a different kind than Ol' Foamy's. I'd say.")

3

SECOND QUALIFICATION:

Apprenticeship

In the making of an Angler, serving an apprenticeship used to mean lowly beginnings. Often, today, a sportsman goes to a fly-fishing or spin-casting school and, in one weekend, graduates into a finished professional. He can whip out line and lay his artificial offering in the water and, once in a while, it's true, he may even evoke a response from a game-fish. An old-timer, on the other hand, instinctively drops his lures over trout, salmon, bass and other species, and experiences ten hits to every one achieved by the weekend wonder.

As the worn witticism is worded, "A fish has one of the lower intelligences among living organisms but a great many so-called intellectual human beings spend a lifetime trying to outwit a poor dumb fish."

So, in our decadent decades, we didn't begin fly-fishing all at once but we gradually worked up to this pristine pastime by starting our angling with telescope rods, level lines, snelled hooks and common earthworms. After a few years passed, we acquired fundamental knowledge about the more productive fish holes (now often called habitat). We learned by experience that heavier gamefishes normally lie in deeper water; that, in streams, they may be at the head of a pool, the tail of a pool, or in riffles, according to where their natural food supply is most abundant at any given time of day and even at any specific period of the year.

We observed fish resting in pools after they had fed in shallower water, perhaps. We automatically placed our offerings in the swirling runs that were formed by the confluence of a cold-water brook and the twisting rush of a river. We tried to drift baits or artificials beneath overhanging banks; to float them against big rocks and waterlogged trees; to seek out sheltered locations that we learned were the lairs of lunkers.

We jotted down small but substantive specificities like: The black-looking water we see from the window of a bush pilot's plane as we circle a wilderness trout pond is called a "spring-hole" and, in hot weather, all the fish in the lake will be lying in that dark, cool area. So, that's where we'll fish.

Perhaps, then, it wasn't a waste of our youth to serve an apprenticeship so lowly as that which included bobbing for eels in the brackish tidal ditches that wander and wind their way to the sea across the marshes of New Hampshire and Maine.

We used to thread those fat worms called nightwalkers on linen sewing line (the kind our mothers used to fasten big buttons on our overalls and jumpers) and keep adding worms until we had a "bob" of them about the size of a baseball. This gob—or bob—of bait was lowered into a hole where fresh water flowed into the marsh stream. The eels would grab onto the bob and we would haul them in with a steady pull, since they refused to let go of the worms even after we had lifted them from the water. Their mouths would be clamped over the linen thread and it sometimes took a minute or two to free them before we dumped the squirming eels into a grain bag.

Once, three of us were having a good night with the snake-like fishes, bagging some two feet and more long. The Depression was upon us and we knew that, skun and cut up into chunks and fried in deep fat and batter, the eels would give us several meals for our families. Maybe not as tasty as scallops but something that would stick to our ribs, notwithstanding.

About midway through our quest for sustenance that evening, the town drunk staggered onto the scene. He slumped down beside us. We grabbed his arms to keep him from sliding into the river and, at that moment, our companion eeler hauled in a three-foot "snake." He freed it carefully and guided the squirming head into the baggy pants of the inebriated newcomer.

Shortly, the beer in our buddy's bladder began to require voiding. He achieved an upright stance and unbuttoned (it was the pre-zipper era), then closed both clammy hands over the wiggling eel. He looked understandably startled as he threw it to the ground.

We were ashamed. The experience had sobered him, we knew. Like the absentminded professor who unbuttoned his vest, took out his necktie and wet his pants, this unfortunate alcoholic was trying to be a good sport. One of our trio was a poultry farmer. He guessed that the drunk had spent his last dime on beer and that his family would go hungry.

"Let's go by my place," he said, putting his arm around the shoulders of the now only slightly wobbling man. "I've got some turkeys dressed out in my cooler and I want you to take one home for those nice kids of yours."

The result was pitiable. The erstwhile butt of our crude humor brushed the tears from his eyes and kept telling us: "I don't deserve your sympathy. Got to straighten out. I'll do it, too, by all that's holy."

To recapture our mood of joviality, we began recounting local happenings that struck us as funny then.

"You know that new family that moved in last month? Took a house on the edge of town, remember? Name is German or Dutch: K-o-o-n-t-z. Old man's name is Bob.

"Well, one of the sons stuck his head in the barber shop the other day and hollered: 'Bob Koontz in here?'

" 'No,' the barber said. 'Just straight haircuts and shaves.' "

One of our gathering places, the barber shop was a retreat where conversations often took an odd twist. I was reminded of the time a lifelong bachelor told us about his plans to get married to a questionable woman—one who looked like she never had taken a bath, who was as old as the aging bachelor and whose morals were lower than a burbot's belly.

"Don't tell me you're going to marry that old hag," the barber expostulated. "Why, she's slept with every man in this town!"

The bachelor sighed. "So what? This ain't a very big town."

Yet we seldom strayed far from the subject of fishing. I had promised to pick some fresh worms for our next eel safari and I couldn't resist putting in my two cents' worth.

"Funny thing, boys. The colder the climate, the faster these worms move. Ever realize we call them night*crawlers* here in New Hampshire, but over the line in Maine, they call them night*walkers* and up in the northern areas they call them night*runners?*

"Funny thing, too," I remembered. "Around some of those mountain streams there aren't any worms in the soil. Not one. Yet the trout will hit a worm every time. Only place I was able to find any a few years ago, up that way, was in a farmer's manure pile and they were the little red worms, not like ours down here near the seacoast."

"I suppose you heard about the boy who was working his way through college, selling boxes of facts," one of my friends interrupted. "Seems he'd go to a house and tell the woman who came to the door that the shoebox under his arm was filled with facts, and she could only satisfy her curiosity by giving him a dollar.

"Then, when she opened the box, she'd cry: 'Why, young man, this is nothing but horse manure.'

"And the boy would agree: 'That's a fact.' "

Then, with due solemnity, we would say goodnight and be on our worthless ways, not realizing then that all experience—even storytelling—was part of our apprenticeship, and that all of this would go into The Making of an Angler.

4

THIRD QUALIFICATION:

Introspection

Some time along the way in life, an individual must look inside himself and decide if his goals are high enough. Is he going to aim for a higher plateau or accept his prosaic lot? In my own case, a forty-hour, five-day week on newspapers theoretically gave me two days for fishing. But there were family and social obligations that frequently cut into my Saturdays and Sundays, so I looked around a bit and finally found a position with the requirement that I promote outdoor recreation to encourage tourism and thus improve the economic life of State of Mainers.

Now I was obligated to take other outdoor writers, photographers, newsreel, radio and television personalities fishing, with the expectation that they would produce material that would ultimately excite vacationers to visit Maine, buy licenses, employ guides, rent watercraft, stay at resort facilities, spend their discretionary income on Maine-made products, and so forth.

This kind of "work" gave me a warm feeling and a legitimate excuse to go fishing far more often than I had in the past.

It seemed to me I had climbed about as high as any honest, freedom-loving American should expect to ascend short of the Hereafter where sleep is unnecessary and I can fish eternally twenty-four hours a day.

Therefore, I've concentrated my introspection on such important matters as those I am about to set down here and haven't searched my soul too often with regard to my niche in society. After all, I didn't want to learn that I was, perhaps, what many of my more ambitious ancestors would have called "a good-for-nothing, lazy S of a B." (Which would have been strong language coming from one of my ancestors.)

As a fishing friend of mine once observed, "I never heard either of your parents say a worse word than bull-nasty. They must have gone through heaven a-flukin'."

Doubtless to cover my embarrassment over such left-handed compliments, I always have been quick to respond with a quickie or two, whatever the subject involved. This time it was Paradise, so I asked him:

"Know why the Gates of Heaven are like a man's pants-fly? Because that's where Ol' Peter hangs out."

He looked at me and seemed to feel it was time to change the subject. So he wondered how water levels in some of our secret fishing lakes were holding up that particular season.

"Water," I said. "They say Winston Churchill always drank Scotch on the rocks, never with water. Once he was in a bar where his preference wasn't known and he was asked, 'Water in your Scotch, Sir?'

" 'No, dammit. No water. Fish eff in it.' "

"They don't, actually," my meticulous friend reminded me.

"That's what the maiden lady asked the fisheries biologist during his address on reproduction of salmon. 'Don't the fish? Er, don't the fish?'

" 'No, lady, they don't.'

" 'Oh,' she sighed. 'The poor fish.'

"Water," I added, "rots leather boots, rusts pipes, floods out cities, drowns people and freezes in the winter. Don't see how fish can stand it."

He decided he'd had enough of this kind of chatter and a deep silence descended on us like a cloud envelops a mountain peak. I thought that still-fishing might be interpreted as an occasion when an angler knew enough to keep his mouth shut, so that's what I did then.

But my thoughts took me back to Fish River Lake in Aroostook County, Maine, on an occasion when several newsmen and I were covering a trip there by half a dozen of the Boston Celtics basketball team. It was early in the spring. Ice still floated in the lake; snow was on the bank and stood deep and white in the woods back of the log camp where we were housed for our stay.

Everybody but me bundled up and, having set up their trolling rods, they rolled into boats forward of each guide and soon were underway, cruising the lake for landlocked salmon or brook trout. ("Perhaps neither," I thought. For it started to snow, the waves were high, and the cold north wind came out of Canada's vastness and whistled mournfully through the evergreens.)

I sat in the cabin alone before a roaring log fire, keeping it going to thaw out the fishermen on their return.

"Trout will be close to shore in weather like this," I thought. "Particularly at this time of year."

If I were fishing from the lake, I would try to cast a streamer fly nearly onto shore, then retrieve it slowly but with short jerks each time it settled on bottom, I decided. But the way the wind was blowing, doubtless it was wise of my friends not to try any such method, since they could quickly hook themselves or one another. Trolling probably was the more sensible decision.

After a while, I put a five-ounce fly rod together and, attaching a reel that carried a heavy sinking line on its spool, I threaded the leader through the guides and bent on a No. 8 Black Ghost streamer fly. The cabin was but a few yards from the lake and I hastened through the snow and made a roll cast that placed the Black Ghost perhaps fifty feet out in the lake. I let it sink to bottom. Then I canted my rod through a crotch of a lakeside tree and ran back into the warm camp.

In ten minutes' time I trotted out to the lake again and, picking up the rod, I yanked hard on the line to activate the sunken streamer fly.

There was a tug and shortly I hauled in a brook trout that, when measured and weighed, was a respectable fourteen inches and nearly two pounds of firm-bodied fish.

Before the boys returned, I had taken another trout of similar size.

I hung them from a cross-log, where they would have to pass them or bump into them, and, thawing out my tackle in front of the fire, I dried it carefully and sat sipping a drink. Soon the cold weather caused the others to return.

"Where the hell did those fish come from?" everybody demanded at once.

They didn't believe me at first (for which I hardly blamed them, as this little trick couldn't be duplicated consistently, that's certain). Yet, since the trout were fresh, and I repeated: "That's the story I made up and that's the one I'm going to stick with," they finally gave me credit and even tried to take more trout by spincasting from shore, between warm-up periods inside.

As we chatted about fishing and basketball, I told them I had occasionally caught lake trout in New Hampshire by using a similar method to that which had snagged the pair of Aroostook brookies that morning.

"When we went ashore to cook lunch, after trolling a red-fin shiner on a lead-core line in any given lake," I said, "we'd sometimes let the bait settle perhaps fifty yards offshore, then unwind line and prop our rod in a spike-holder up on the bank near our cooking site.

"Not always but occasionally, a lake trout would take the shiner bait and we'd let him run with it for a minute or two. When the reel stopped, we knew the trout was swallowing the shiner, so we'd set the hook and reel him ashore."

Just to show our readers how tricky we were with promotional pictures, too, here is one I cooked up next afternoon.

The boys had awakened to a warm, sunshiny spring day, after all of the freezing cold the day before. Fish had cooperated and they had a lake trout in their catch that weighed about five pounds. (These are called "togue" in Maine.)

I persuaded a guide to nail a big boat net in a birch tree on an open point of land. Then I asked Bob Cousy and Bill Sharman to pose under the net-basket, holding the togue above it as if they were making a score with a Maine fish in a staged basketball game. Both men were at the peaks of their careers and the national wire services sent that picture from coast to coast.

There were, then, rewarding experiences that resulted from my decision to mature into nothing much except a fun-loving fisherman. The stories told around the log camp fireplace in the evenings were a bonus, too.

Once, five of the Celtics were on a barnstorming tour of northern New England in their off-season, they recalled. Crossing from one city to another over a country road they got behind a truck. They were late for their scheduled appearance and they blew the horn frantically but the truck driver didn't budge from the center of the road.

Finally, in desperation, they took their lives in their hands and passed the truck on the soft shoulder of the narrow road.

Then they stopped their car in front of the truck.

Two burly men came stomping up to the car. The shortest team member. Bob Cousy, stepped out—and he was six feet tall. Then, successively, the other four players unwound their long legs and took positions beside Cousy. Six-four, six-six, six-eight and seven feet tall, the players glared at the truckers.

"You boys looking for trouble?" they rumbled.

"Never saw such apologetic truck drivers," they remembered, chuckling.

5

Evanescent Evenings

Salmon and trout seekers long have romanticized a time of day when something known as "The Evening Hatch" is supposed to occur. Yet several habits block us from being on lake or wading stream at precisely the right time to take advantage of this brief period. Chief among these is the cocktail hour—rarely as brief as sixty minutes. It is too late too soon and we might as well stay in for dinner.

To make every minute of all-too-short fishing trips count, we cast intensely all day and perhaps decide that since action has been slow it won't necessarily improve when the sun sets.

Finally, if we swallow a couple of quick ones and rush away to fish, the alcohol, likely as not, affects our timing (can't seem to hook one!) and mysteriously puts snarls in our leaders, breaks off flies and blinds our eyes when we try to tie on another fly.

In The Making of an Angler, then, a graduate might re-schedule his social timetables. That is, if he is going to catch sun-shy, elusive, leader-timid trout and selectively feeding salmon with any consistency.

Like farmers, a fisherman should begin his day an hour at least before sunrise. Then he might return to camp or home, mix a hot buttered rum if so inclined, and follow up with a hearty breakfast. He might sleep until lunch, or relax other-wise, according to his mood. The cocktail hour could be en-joyed with friends at noon. Not ever in the evening.

A serious angler would prepare for what is normally the peak fishing period, from sunset to dark, well in advance of that time. An hour before rises are anticipated, he should be at streamside or within casting distance of a known trout and salmon "hole" on lake or pond, patiently waiting and closely watching for the first insects to hatch, for the initial slurps and splashes of feeding gamefish. Then he can choose pat-terns resembling naturals.

He will have tied flies to leaders so that he can change tip-pet and all, should the need occur when it gets too dark to thread a tippet quickly into the dimly obscured eye of a tiny dry fly.

His lines will be stretched to take out the kinks, his leaders straightened by pulling them through a piece of rubber. Knots tested. All made ready.

Even so, he may not take a trout or snare a salmon; he may only excite a few to hit; but, if ever he is going to be pre-sent at a performance when nature's symphony is played to the full and the soul-stirring splashes of feeding fish harmo-nize with night-singing birds, cheeping tree-toads, crying, lonely loons, wind whispering and dying in the trees—then that time is evening, evanescent, mysterious prelude to the blackness of night.

Sometimes, I have learned, fish begin feeding as the sun sinks. On other occasions I have not had a strike until the last lingering minute of the day.

Once, on a northern Maine pond, a friend and I were fish-ing from a canoe. None of those magical, pulse-quickening dimples showed on the calm surface. It was a rather long paddle back to camp. He took his rod apart and bagged his reel. Shrugging his shoulders, he indicated that we might as well quit and hope for another, more fruitful day.

We were anchored on a rocky-bottomed shoal just off a small wooded island, a spot that produced trout more often than not in the evening at this time of year. I didn't want to quit yet but yielded to his wishes. However, I left my fly rod set up, its tip pointing back over the stern of the canoe, as I pulled anchor and began stroking the paddle softly and easily to keep us underway.

We had slid along several hundred yards and now came parallel to a rocky point. Big boulders, I knew, lay well under the surface and extended out into the lake. No danger of hitting them, so I dipped the blade and drove the canoe ahead more smartly. Just then I saw mayflies hovering in the air at eye-level, and more of them rising from the water.

"A late hatch this evening," I said.

"Too late," my companion observed.

Even as he spoke, I dropped the paddle, picked up my rod and made a short cast to where a trout had surfaced. When the big dry No. 8 Royal Coachman Wulff kissed the circle left by the trout, I had a smashing strike and was fast to a heavy fish. It took me five minutes to bring it to net. I judged its weight at a pound and a half, at least.

The canoe had drifted. Passing my rod to my friend, I urged: "Watch for a rise and cast!"

He answered: "With my luck today . . ."

"There's one! Cast!"

He did, and another trout drove for the Coachman and was fast to it before either of us could do anything wrong. Paddling slowly now, I returned to the reef where my first trout had shown. The water was boiling with feeding fish. We took turns casting, and in short order boated another good one apiece.

"For breakfast," I told him.

Suddenly it was too dark to mark the rises. Yet those trout were splashing in a frenzy and I thought we might have experienced strikes regardless of where we placed our casts. But we didn't stay. Somehow, I believe, the real fun in this kind of fishing is to drop a dry fly on the edge of a dimpling circle made when a trout comes up and to have it return for the artificial.

That, to me, is what it's all about.

At no other time of day is this possible to the extent it is in the final hour before full night.

Yes, I, too, have taken trout at noon and under a bright sun by casting dry or wet flies in known fish holes. The rapids and slicks in rivers that partially obscure leaders, small waves on lakes to hide otherwise apparent tackle—these conditions make for reasonably good action. But, oh, those evening fly hatches, when it's still light enough over water to place an offering accurately.

On another wilderness lake a year or two ago, I dropped in by float plane a couple of hours before dark. The fishing lodge was owned by a man whose love for taking trout and salmon on dry flies equalled my own. We were automatically out on the lake in time for the evening hatches.

We cast a variety of patterns just off the mouth of an incoming stream, at a point where the shallows shelved deeply and where, we knew, trout might lie between feeding forays on the gravel bar above their lair. There was a comparatively light hatch of mayflies which we ultimately were able to match with sufficient semblance to take small brook trout. None of them was heavy enough to make the action exciting.

"Perhaps larger trout are lying in deeper water," my friend suggested. He moved the aluminum boat a few feet at a time while I cast. All at once a fish swirled at my fly—but didn't take it. We anchored there and began to cast.

I noticed a small insect on the surface. Even though the larger mayflies continued to drift upward and to float on the lake, they were not being taken readily, it seemed to me. So I changed flies. There was just light enough to outline the eye of a No. 16 black gnat for my tippet. I cast it toward the spot where the fish had swirled at the other fly.

It barely hit the water when a salmon came up, out and

down on the barb in a wild series of motions that thrilled me to my very core. He was on!

Primarily with trout in mind, I had brought out a Hardy cane rod weighing 2¼ ounces and measuring but six feet in length. So I had my hands full.

The salmon stripped line down to the backing. I kept tension on him but just barely, not wanting the leader to part. He jumped and dove repeatedly. Bright and silvery in late summer coloration, vigorous from his life in cold water, he was a beautiful antagonist.

It took a while to bring him in. We guessed his weight at four pounds. Then I let him go.

"Tomorrow evening, if conditions are like this, we'll have a session with these babies," I said. "And you know, I think I'll stick with this light rod, too. Man, do I ever love to cast to a feeding fish, have him take it that way and turn out to be a real fighter."

"Anglers have been trolling for salmon all season in this lake," my friend said, "but they've only taken a few fish. I've seen schools of salmon on their spawning beds every fall. I know they're here."

"They're spectacular any time, but on a little dry fly evenings like this . . . I can hardly wait until tomorrow afternoon."

6

FOURTH QUALIFICATION:

Humility

About the time an angler decides he has achieved perfection, he runs into a guide or two who quickly disillusion him and gently ease him back down the ladder of fishing status without seeming to push him around but only to prove how much more skillful they are themselves.

Long ago, I made this a rule: When fishing in unfamiliar waters, always employ a guide for at least a day or two. Then, keep on asking his advice until he breaks down and discloses a secret trick on what to fish with and, more importantly, where to cast, troll or bait-fish, as the case may be.

Just as you and I employ a mechanic for intricate jobs and leave the solutions to him, so we should recognize that an experienced local fishing guide knows more about catching the gamefishes he has grown up with than we can hope to learn in one easy session.

For example, another outdoor writer and I were fishing for smallmouth black bass in eastern Maine one early summer day. Our guide ran his outboard motor and slowed down whenever we indicated what we intuitively felt were logical places to cast popping bugs and streamer flies. And we did take a few fish, but none worthy of our cameras.

Just before going ashore at a cooking site, I remarked that we had hoped to photograph a couple of three-pound bass or larger—being brought to net and, later, being filleted and fried over an open fire. The guide stopped his big canoe, except for the wind-drift. He picked up a short spin-casting rod that was rigged with a monofilament line and two feather jigs, one on the end of the line and the second jig about eighteen inches above the first. The terminal jig was black, and feathers on the other one were bright yellow.

He dropped the rig over the side and, as it touched bottom, he started working it quickly up and down. Within minutes the rod bowed sharply and he hoisted a big smallmouth into the canoe. In hardly any time at all he brought a second three-pounder aboard.

"May not be quite as sporting as cork-popping," he chuckled, "but it sure as hell works, huh?"

Slightly stunned, we nodded in unison.

On another occasion I was fishing the evening hatch for brook trout in northern Maine. An elderly guide had poled us upstream in his canoe to a spot on Chemquassabamticook Brook where two forks in the shallow river converged to make an alluring pool. I worked the pool over with a variety of dry flies and took and released a few small brookies.

Our time was short. I asked the guide, "Any suggestions?"

"Do you have a small Brown Wulff?"

"Yes."

"Forget the pool," he advised. "See that rock on the bank just below us? Cast as close to the stream side of it as you can. Water swirls against it there and it's a lot deeper than it looks from here."

There wasn't any wind and I was able to place the No. 12 Wulff precisely where he had suggested. Immediately a twelve-inch fish rose and smashed the fly hard.

Repeated casts brought action from fish of similar size on almost every offering.

We were on an Allagash Wilderness Waterway canoeing, camping and fishing trip, and I kept enough of the firm-fleshed brook trout for our evening meal.

As we continued on our river and pond trek during the days that followed, this same guide would stop his canoe every hour or two and tell me precisely where to lay a fly to catch trout. We went past many locations that looked ideal to me but I learned that the guide paused only at the truly productive spots. My astonishment and respect for this knowledgeable man increased during the hundred-mile trek.

He told me modestly that he had been born beside the river, had worked for years on log drives there and had learned to read the waters from such close association.

He not only knew the lairs of trout but rarely did his canoe even graze the hidden boulders and sunken logs in the hazardous pitches along our way. That sort of thing can bestow the gift of humility on an angler; it's a helpful lesson.

During my progress toward maturity as an angler I have known many guides in many places and with but a few exceptions I have found them to be similarly alert to their immediate locale, if not the entire state they lived in. Some of them have knocked in the head theories held by elite aristocrats of the angle and I am reluctant to destroy the lofty versions of how, why and when we practice the more pristine piscatorial procedures inherited from our gentleman ancestors.

Take the custom of fly-fishing upstream. As tough as it may be to buck currents and snags, we defend ourselves by pointing out that fish lie with their hungry mouths open for insects washing downriver naturally. And we argue that the waters above are undisturbed by our progress.

"Indians used to spread nets near the lower reaches of brooks and then a crowd of them would wade downstream, making all the commotion they could, to drive gamefish into their nets. They smoked the heavy hauls for winter use." One old guide, who believes this is the origin of our ethical upriver fly-fishing, adds:

"Streams are so crowded nowadays that smart fishermen work very slowly up the brooks, knowing those angling above them will drive the trout and bass down to them. That's all."

"Yeah," another guide agrees. "And if there aren't any fishermen upriver, and nobody's watching, some fly casters will heave a rock or two upstream to frighten the fish into swimming down where they can cast to them."

I said: "This is heresy."

"Worse than that," an old-timer added solemnly.

Other guides have debased the phraseology we use to dignify our art. Like: "A fly tier is somebody who never heard of buttons or zippers." . . . Or "A fly-fisherman is somebody who fumbles with his fly in cold weather, trying to find a certain little thing."

"Cork-popping is not only opening wine bottles but bouncing cork-bodied bugs on water for bass."

"A troller is an angler who believes in trolls."

"Tackle can mean a three-hundred pound football player or a half-ounce piece of tonkin cane."

"A rod can be a pistol or a high-class name for a bamboo pole, but anybody who calls a fly rod a pole will be blackballed when he applies for membership in any angling club."

"A spoon is an eating utensil and we try to persuade gamefish to bite one."

Just as words can be bent to suit a man's fancy, so can the way he sees a fishing situation or any situation. A guide's wit has more than once helped me take myself less seriously and reflect that my way of looking at things is only one of many. "We can get things mixed up without half trying," a guide remarked to me. "Like the time the old man of the forest married a girl of eighteen and took her into his cabin for the winter. Their nearest neighbors, twenty miles down a logging road, were a couple with opposite ages, a man of twenty-one married to a woman old enough to be his mother.

"The two couples would get together on Saturday nights to drink a little beer and play cards. As the winter went on, the old man's young bride looked better and better to the twenty-one-year-old, and she began to feel the same kind of stirrings," the guide continued. "But of course, the old man and the old woman thought too much of themselves to dream that maybe something was up between their young spouses.

"Finally, the young fellow whispered his love in the willing ears of the girl and they proceeded to pour beer into their doddering partners until the old man and the old woman were groggy. But they missed the youngsters shortly and the old man staggered to an adjoining bunk-room and called to his neighbor's ancient wife:

" 'Take a look, Maggie.'

"She came over and saw the young pair in bed.

" 'Ain't that a sight!' the old man cried. 'Young feller in bed with my wife. He's so drunk he thinks he's *me!*' "

I have found guides' stories so entertaining at times that even if fish didn't strike I still thoroughly enjoyed the wild woods-and-waters tales.

Once, an elderly giant of the evergreens described the problems he faced when he started a fishing lodge deep in the northwoods of Maine.

"In the early 1900's," he recalled, "there weren't any trained fishing guides and I simply employed some of the older woodsmen to paddle and pole canoes and cook noon meals outdoors for our guests. The language of those loggers was colorful. It didn't matter so much until sportsmen from the cities started bringing their wives into camp. Then I told my woodsmen-guides to watch their words. If they had to use profanity, they'd do better to keep silent. Some of them became like stone images and others just mumbled short answers when a lady asked them simple questions.

"In those early days, most of the gals were awful prim and stuffy. Haughty, too, sometimes. Now and then it was a relief to come across one who had enough humility underneath all that whalebone to laugh at herself and admit she was just as human as us ordinary folks."

The wife of a prominent New York banker once arrived in camp with her spouse, the old man remembered. She was stout, solemn, dignified. "We gave her two good men to serve as guides," he told me. "They helped her into a twenty-foot canoe and she squatted in the middle in a canoe seat while the guides kneeled in stern and bow to paddle her around a small lake.

"She was corseted in one of those tight whalebone harnesses they used to wear and she had at least three petticoats under a black silk dress. She had a shawl around her neck and shoulders and a sweater over the whole works, of course. The boys were pretty shy and they guarded their tongues in front of all that dignity. They broiled steaks over a fire at noon, along with some trout she'd caught. There was plenty of coffee, homemade bread and big slices of apple pie and country cheese. The boys said she kept right up with them when it came to stowing away the food.

"They had a chance to relieve themselves on the excuse of gathering firewood to leave at the campsite. But the woman stayed right beside the fire until they helped her back into the canoe for some more fishing.

"Those early guides believed in giving an honest day's work," he said, proudly. "So it was nearly dark when they finally paddled up to the landing in front of our main camp. By then, I guess their portly female 'sport' was straining her corset laces, but she still stood on her dignity—or sat on it,

anyway. She seemed to be glued to her canoe seat. They could see she was uncomfortable, so each man took hold of a hand and forearm and steadied her as they heaved her into an upright position. That was just too much for her. She'd probably been thinking about her favorite home remedy for gas ever since that noon meal, and the safety valve was bound to blow. One of the boys said it sounded like the crack of a moose gun on a frosty morning.

"Now she was accepted into the woodsmen's fraternity. And now, she showed her true sporting colors beneath all that solemn surface flummery. One of the men slapped her on the back as he cried: 'Good for another mile, b'God! Good for another mile!'

" 'What's that?' she snapped.

" 'That's what we allus say on the trail when somebody lets a good one like that. Good for another mile; you're good for another mile!'

"You know," the old guide said, "that woman laughed until she almost cried.

" 'When we go fishing tomorrow, boys, I want you to tell me what a woman is supposed to do this far away from a bathroom.'

" 'Ma'am,' the woodsman told her solemnly, 'these woods is just full of ass-high logs. When you feel the need, you just say so and we'll show you an ass-high log before you can get your pants down. Ain't nothing cleaner nor more comfortable than an ass-high log, providin' you pick one with smooth bark.' "

7

FIFTH QUALIFICATION:

Memory Bank

Buried in the subconscious are magical tricks that fooled gamefish on at least one occasion but that an angler has failed to use consistently because they were so far from normally accepted fishing practices as to make him appear eccentric if he dragged them out in front of fishing companions.

For example, a system of trolling streamer flies when angling for landlocked salmon long ago was conceived in Maine and this method has been used by most salmon-seekers ever since. The sportsmen lock two fly rods in holders on either side of the boat. These rods point only slightly toward the stern. Level sinking flylines and long sinking leaders are fed off the reels, and single- or tandem-hooked flies are on the leader terminals. No weight is added, as the idea is to troll the flies just barely under the surface. These two side lines are trolled about thirty yards behind the boat.

Another similarly rigged outfit is used in a stern rod-holder, so the fly is towed in the wake of the motor. This time the fly is trolled much closer—no more than eight or ten yards astern—as the idea is to attract those landlocked salmon that come up into the motor wake, as they frequently seem to do.

When salmon strike and the reels sing, experienced trollers do not pick up the rods immediately, as the temptation to yank the fly away from the fish is a human reaction. There are many short strikes, but those who practice this kind of fishing declare that landlocks either hook themselves or go free and that grabbing the rod is a pretty certain way of losing the action, anyhow. When a rod stays bowed for a minute, then it is taken from its holder and the salmon is carefully played to net.

Used to paddling slowly in Northern lakes, old guides advised their "sports" to jerk on the line occasionally to give life to a fly or live, sewed-on smelt, as the case might be. Those old-timers were reluctant to accept outboard motors when they first became popular. The suggestion from so-called "authorities" that more salmon would strike if a boat or canoe was motored along at five miles an hour, met with the disdain of early professional guides.

Once, when a sportsman insisted that a motor be used and that landlock fishing be done with the three-rod system described above, a white-whiskered old man did as he was told without comment but he boiled inwardly.

To make things worse, all the other guides came in with limits of landlocks for their clients and the motorized old-timer was ribbed unmercifully for his failure to take fish. This gloomy situation lasted a week. Then, a foolish salmon did hit the stern-trolled fly and the old man picked it up and slammed it down on the dock in full view of his compatriots.

"Well," he exclaimed, "one of the bastards finally caught up with us!"

Many years ago I was fishing for landlocked salmon at Moosehead Lake, Maine's largest inland body of water. My guide was an Indian. The way we fished, I asked him to hold one fly rod between his knees while he paddled his big lake-type canoe and, from the bow seat, I cast a streamer fly in toward shore as we paralleled the curving rocky line of the land. I took good-sized speckled trout, and an occasional landlocked salmon would follow my cast fly out, drop back and strike the streamer being trolled by the guide. Then he would pass the rod to me so I could play the salmon.

We kept one or two trout for cooking at noon. The landlocks were running small for such a big lake and all of them went back during the day's fishing. I was in camp with a group of New England outdoor writers and we all were looking for some of the landlocks for which Moosehead Lake was then famous—fish of at least five pounds and, occasionally, ten, twelve and fifteen pounds. (The world's record for the species is 22½ pounds, and this landlocked salmon came from Sebago Lake, Maine, in the early 1900's.)

We had an informal, state-sponsored association for anglers who took trophy fish of the various species from Maine waters. The group was known as the "One That Didn't Get Away Club." Qualifications were strict and, in the days of which I am writing, a landlock had to weigh fifteen pounds to make a sportsman eligible for membership. It has since dropped to eight pounds for salmon, and only a few of this weight are caught nowadays in Maine.

In any event, nobody in our group had caught a landlock of impressive size, and our trip was soon to end. That evening, before dark, my Indian guide called me aside and asked: "Have you got a casting reel with a hundred yards or more of line on it?"

"Yes."

"Get it and come with me."

I fastened the reel to a short boat rod, threaded the line through the guides and tied on a long leader, then a Gray Ghost streamer fly that he chose from my book. The pattern was on a No. 4 long-shank hook.

The lake was calm. Not a ripple stirred its glasslike surface. (Waves, at least small waves, are thought to be a must
for successful landlocked-salmon action.)

The guide paddled out into the lake, farther from shore
than we ordinarily fished in the spring months. He told me to
feed out line until eighty or ninety yards took the Gray
Ghost away back of the canoe. In the light of the setting sun
we could see the streamer floating on the lake. Within a few
minutes the guide told me, "When I give the word, you yank
hard on that line. Real hard, now! And hold your seat, because I'm going to dig the paddle in and jump the canoe
ahead."

As I followed his instructions, I looked back and saw a big
salmon leap out of water. The line was slack for a second and
as I gasped, "Look at that!" I realized the landlock was fast
to my fly.

With the skillful handling of the canoe by the guide, I was
able to bring the fish to net within a few minutes of the most
exciting action I ever had experienced.

The fish weighed six pounds—not the heaviest I had ever
taken but, after the small ones of the past several days, this
certainly was a trophy landlock. Back at the lodge, the others
wanted to know all the details, but I was sworn to secrecy by
the guide. He had explained to me how he knew the
salmon's secret ways.

"When they don't strike well in the daytime, it means the
heavier salmon are feeding in the early morning about sunrise, after dark or now, just before the last sun rays leave the
water. I've checked during the past couple of days, and last
night about the time we caught that big one I saw big schools
of smelts breaking the surface. I knew gamefish were chasing
them. But on such smooth water I realized we put both the
baitfish and the salmon down if we came too close to them.
So—the long line.

"The jerk on the fly and digging in the paddle were to attract attention to what looked like a crippled minnow.
Worked, huh?"

Along with similar trickery, this experience went into my

memory bank and it stayed there, unused for several years because, by relying on the more common method of trolling for landlocks in the spring, I wasn't skunked often enough to dredge my mind for the unusual practices.

Then, here I was with three friends at East Grand Lake, a long, meandering body of water that lies on the Maine-New Brunswick boundary—the home of lake trout of creditable weight and of landlocked salmon that can grow to six, eight and more pounds. We had fished East Grand for three days without a salmon strike. We told one another that this was typical: Either the landlocks hit or they didn't. They certainly weren't hitting now.

Two of the boys had tried trolling deep with lead-core lines and sewed-on smelts. One had fished near the surface with a variety of lures. But I had stayed with single-hook streamer flies. We hadn't even caught small fish of any species. We had rented a housekeeping camp, and after supper on our last day there I suddenly suggested that one of the men take me back out to fish until dark. "You run the motor, I'll catch the salmon," I said, laughing.

He was agreeable but doubtful.

I rigged the casting line and reel on a fly rod. Again, attached to my long leader was a Gray Ghost streamer. As we paralleled the shoreline we had fished for three days fruitlessly, I fed off line until about a hundred yards lay between us and the fly. My companion watched, smiling.

Then, I yanked hard on the line, and a fine salmon smashed the streamer and broke water. I shouted in glee. My friend asked, incredulously, "Is that your fly he hit way back there?"

The rod singing, the reel whining and line falling back even more, I yelled: "Shut off your motor. Quick."

He did better, realizing I was down to the final few turns on my reel spool; he turned the boat and allowed me to retrieve line. Soon we had the salmon thrashing in the boat bottom.

Before dark, we took our limits of landlocks—ten pounds apiece was the legal allowance then. We had two that weighed seven and a half and eight pounds, respectively. Maine laws allow an additional gamefish provided the first ones caught do not exceed the aggregate weight permissible, so we could take another salmon regardless of its weight. All four salmon struck flies ninety to a hundred yards back of the boat.

Our friends were amazed when we came in with those husky landlocks. We had agreed not to tell them the way we had fished, holding them in suspense for a time.

Next day, since two of us had our limits, we ran the motors on a pair of boats for our buddies. Again, by midafternoon not a fish had heeded lures of any kind.

My companion on this occasion asked me how we had caught the big salmon on the previous evening and I finally broke down and showed him my method. He vowed I was pulling his leg but we hadn't gone half a mile before a nice landlock took the way-back streamer fly. I handed the rod to my buddy and he brought in a five-pounder. Convinced, he trolled the same way for another two hours without getting a strike.

The offbeat tricks are like that. Sometimes they work and on other trips nothing will catch fish—including all the magic from one's memory bank.

8

SIXTH QUALIFICATION:

Craftsmanship

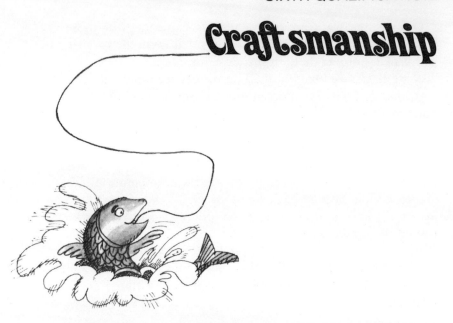

Occasionally, during periods when fishing action slows down, I find myself looking at the hands of my angling companions and thinking how they obey the mind and will of man. Heavily knotted and veined hands clutching oars or paddles; muscular hands with hairy backs pulling in anchors, then grasping the wheel of a cabin cruiser and guiding us along through fog, rain or springtime sleet and snow. Hands that incredibly can be trained to knot the finest leader and to fashion from fur, feathers and hair a fishing fly so tiny that it must be magnified through a glass as it is assembled.

I search my mind and see my father's hands with deep cracks in the skin and into the flesh itself, a result of shingling a roof in below-zero New England weather. I shudder as he melts beeswax and pours it hot and steaming into the raw openings to seal them against further exposure on the morrow.

I remember my grandfather telling me how he was lost in the fog many miles off Newfoundland when, along with another trawler, they failed to locate their mother vessel after hauling their gear and stowing it in their big bank dory. So they set their course and rowed to the Canadian island, despite snow, high seas, fog, freezing cold, hunger and thirst.

"We knew we had to keep going. If we quit for even an hour it would be the end. At the last we dipped our hands in the spray and froze them to the oars. It was the only way."

Fortunately, they were sighted by Newfoundland fishermen before their hands froze completely and shut off circulation, else they would have lost them to a surgeon.

His hands could fashion gill nets, lobster-trap heads, jigs, swordfish irons. And they could grasp knives and other tools to shape such lifelike waterfowl decoys that ducks would stool to them, chattering and quacking and seeking vocal response from the cedar blocks.

To qualify as a complete angler, one should train his hands, his arms and, indeed, his whole body, not only to create fishing lures and flies but to execute casts automatically and accurately. A fisherman's hands should not shake even after his third martini, since it is unpardonable to spill good liquor. His hands should pour the exact quantity of dark and light alcohol in hot buttered rums, without resorting to the use of measures. (The trick is to be liberal with the rum. Then nothing can go wrong.)

Yes, hands are important in angling and socializing.

One old guide never uses his hands to swat mosquitoes, nevertheless. "Kill one and a thousand more will come to its funeral," he believes.

I am especially attractive to insects of all kinds. On several occasions I have been made ill by black flies, those scourges of the woods and waters that bite without pain but leave poisonous itching and burning blemishes on anglers like me. I can stand on a dock beside a dozen other people and just

about every black fly in the air will buzz and bite me, ignoring my companions. This is true despite the fact that I spend more time outdoors than many others are privileged to do. I have tried everything from baby oil to the deterrents compounded by the armed forces. They all help a little but none completely. So, when anybody asks me, "What do you do about these damned flies?" I say: "It helps to swear. The worse they are, the fouler the oaths should be. It's an acquired skill, like matching the hatch."

Sometimes alcohol can help, too, but only if used judiciously. Once I saw this demonstrated by a visiting photographer. We had been fishing and picture-taking in northwestern Maine for about a week. My companion had imbibed very heavily each evening after our daily assignments and his nerves were on edge. So much so that I was apprehensive he might crack up.

On the way out of the woods, I lowered the car windows, as the day was warm and the sun shone brightly. He shivered. "These trees give me claustrophobia! The silence is maddening."

I reached down to turn on the car radio. But he suddenly screamed and squirmed and clutched himself by the groin and, as I stopped the car in horror, he leaped out and jumped up and down like a man possessed, all the while emitting a shower of explosive oaths.

He loosened his belt and, still screaming and cursing, he took his pants off and shook them like Betsy is said to have waved the flag in front of her old gray head.

I left the motor running and my side door open, ready to make my instant escape if he became more violent. But he calmed down a bit, although still clutching himself desperately.

"Man, you startled me," I said. "That screaming."

"You'd scream, too, if a bee stung you where that one stung me!" he cried. "Let's get out of here. Lousy woods. Everything is against human life here. How do you stand it, anyhow?"

I dug out a travel bar. "Here, rub a little alcohol on the sting. Not too much, now. Best medicine is taken internally."

Shortly, he was singing and asking me when we could schedule another trip.

Despite such beneficial reactions to liquor, I have made it a rule personally not to imbibe while fishing, driving, taking pictures and doing any essential activity. Evenings in camp, a little can loosen inhibitions and give life a rosy hue. At other times booze can kill, as we all know.

Once a friend of mine had been bass fishing with a buddy of his, he recalls. They had had a ten-day bout with liquor and jollity and were returning home from Downeast Maine over a roller-coaster highway (Route 9) known as the airline road. In those days, the dips and little hillocks were so abrupt that a car would speed into a hollow and, when bouncing over the rise above, the wheels would seem to leave the earth and the vehicle to sail through the air momentarily. Country drivers called these places "Thank-you-Marms" and thrill-hungry youngsters would take them at the highest speed possible.

Well, my friend and his companion were really hung over. The driving was blind, as morning fog filled the air from ground to treetop. They proceeded at a snail's pace. All at once the driver started in terror, he recalls. He glanced at his buddy and saw that his face was chalk-white.

"Do you see it?" he cried.

"Yes. If you do, too, it must be there. Both of us wouldn't get the D.T.'s simultaneously."

They were looking at an elephant. It appeared to be floating through the fog toward them. The driver pulled into a ditch beside the road and shortly a flatbed truck passed them. The fog had completely hidden the truck and only the "flying" elephant could be seen. The tusked monster was being transported to a carnival across the St. Croix River in New Brunswick, Canada.

"Neither of us had a drink for six months afterwards," my friend told me. "If that elephant had been pink, I never would have imbibed again."

It was another elephant that created a situation for a writer who had come to Maine many years ago, looking for local color for his fishing book. The writer was known as extremely careful with his money. An unkind person might

have called him a tightwad. Two or three of his friends came to Maine with him to fill in as models for pictures and to enjoy the good bass fishing. They generously paid for rooms, meals and entertainment while the writer kept his wallet sealed during a two-week stay.

There was a small circus in a nearby village and on the last day the group stopped by for a bit of diversion. They separated from their writer pal and were discussing his niggardly mannerisms as they came to an enclosure that contained a big bull elephant. The attendant was cleaning up the area, a sight that was pure inspiration to one of the boys. It may be that an angler's craftsmanship includes a certain deviousness which can be summoned up to fool a fish or shape a prank, as the need arises. And so the visiting anglers gave the caretaker a tip to help play a joke on their friend.

The writer was an ardent home gardener and, when they took him to the elephant cage, the man was still shovelling up after his huge charge. He told them:

"Too bad to waste this. Nothing in the world makes roses grow like elephant dung. Better than hen and sheep manure. Beats horse droppings all hollow."

The writer swallowed the bait. "Could I have a bagful? I grow roses back home and I'd certainly like to try this elephant dung. If it's as good as you say, maybe I could get some from other circuses occasionally."

The attendant told him: "Just happen to have a big canvas bag. Glad to give you all you want for a dollar.

He went after his car while the grounds-keeper filled a sack. It took two of them to lift the five-foot-high container into the trunk of the writer's car.

The others had driven up together but the writer, typically, had come alone and was returning the same way, not to overload his tires!

After he left for his home in Boston, his buddies called the police in Massachusetts, gave his registration number and a description of his car and told the authorities that they were suspicious the writer had a body in his car trunk.

He was stopped as he crossed the state line, ordered from his automobile, frisked and taken to a police station for questioning, after being told to raise his trunk cover.

When they demanded what he had in the bag and he told them, "Elephant manure," they called in a police psychiatrist who ordered him to open the canvas sack.

As he exposed the contents to view, a policeman exclaimed, "Be damned! Looks like dung. Smells like dung. Guess it *is* dung. *Could* have come from an elephant."

He asked them who had informed on him. They said the message had come by telephone, anonymously. He suspected his fishing friends but couldn't prove it.

"And after all I've done for them!" he exclaimed virtuously.

9

Piscatorial Paternity

Sentimentalism was frowned on among the males in our family. My father was stern, unbending, remote. His heart was tender but he never "wore it on his sleeve," as an old-time saying went. We never embraced. Kissing was reserved for our mother. Growing boys shook hands. A firm grip was evidence of manhood.

I expect I passed this attitude on to my own sons. In their youth they may have thought of me as "a cold fish." We enjoyed outdoor sports individually. I had acquaintances and business contacts with whom I went fishing and hunting; my three sons were more often afield and on the water with boys of their own ages.

In comparatively recent years we find occasions to make trips together, nevertheless. One son is an enthusiastic duck hunter. Another is devoted to ice fishing. A third has told me he would rather cast flies for trout than do anything else on earth.

This is the son whose bride came to Maine twenty years ago to "get acquainted with her husband's family" (my wife and me). Then residents of New Hampshire, they now live in Connecticut.

She was telling us about their sincere efforts to establish themselves independently; how they were saving for this and that and everything needed in their modest home. Our son, she said, was working hard and she knew they would make it but the going was painfully slow. Then the telephone rang. It was her call. She talked and nodded and turned at intervals to relay the news to my wife and me. All at once, she swore.

"He got his bonus. Said he bought something *we both* would enjoy! The S.O.B.! Do you know what he spent that bonus on?"

I guessed, "A fly rod?"

"A fishing boat! Can you imagine? *A boat!* As much as we need furniture. A boat! That S.O.B.!"

"Alice," my wife said mildly, "you might as well get used to it. If you're going to live with anyone who grew up in this family, you might as well learn that fishing and hunting come first."

I was shamefaced. I mumbled that his enthusiasm for outdoor sports could make him a better mate in the long run.

"You know," I told her, "I've worked hard to make a better living financially so I could afford to fish and provide for my family too. If it weren't for fishing, I would have had only a single goal, just to pile up the old lucre."

"Well, we could use a lot more of the filthy stuff until we get our feet on the ground," she answered grimly.

I could see that my son was going to catch hell when she returned home.

Time has tempered her steel but not his fondness for fly-fishing. She encourages him to make an occasional trip "up north" now and he fishes the Housatonic River every evening when he is at home in New Milford.

A mutual friend invited my son and me to visit his company's lodge in northern Maine not long ago. The time was late July-early August. We were to fly in on a float plane one Monday and return the following weekend. But the weather turned unfavorable and we found it necessary to drive two hundred miles, then be picked up and taken sixty miles across northern Maine in a panel truck over logging roads.

We slowed now and then to allow half-grown ruffed grouse to cross the gravel byways or let a moose amble ungracefully into a swamp or a beautiful buck deer pose for our cameras on the edge of a stand of spruce and fir. I thought how lucky we were to have communion in our mutual fondness for such simple things in life.

It is so easy to become maudlin in paternity, I told myself. I guessed none of my sons knew of the long-ago scribbling I had done on the occasion of my first progeny. How had that gone?

> "This is my son:
> Again I have been born,
> And all the failures,
> All obscurants of life
> Are past. Obliterated.
> In this rebirth
> All innocence shines
> Unblemished."

So now, as I heard this second son exclaim about the wildlife in the deep North Woods; as I saw his eyes follow every bend in the numerous streams we crossed on our way into camp; as I read his thoughts ("There just have to be trout in all these brooks and rivers—lying in wait for a well-offered dry fly!") I lived again as I was at his more youthful age.

Our guide, a longtime friend of mine, stopped the truck beside a small lake, which was fed by one of the sparkling brooks that coursed under a log bridge, perhaps halfway in to our destination.

"In the old days," he told us, grinning, "we used to pause at what were then known as 'tea-and-pee shops' so the whole family could intake and output a little liquid, according to their personal needs. I've got half a dozen cans of cold beer here in a portable refrigerator and there are plenty of trees to water, if anybody is so inclined.

"Meanwhile," he looked at my son, "you might want to rig up a fly rod and make a few casts from shore just where this stream empties into that lake. Should be a trout or two feeding there this time of day."

I was proud of the way this man from Connecticut roll-cast a treated Grasshopper out into the current of that wilderness inlet; of how he lifted his arm quickly but gently when a fish swirled under the floating fly.

He lowered the butt of his two-ounce cane rod and the tip bowed and quivered like something come alive. He looked back to see if we knew he had one on. Sipping the cold amber beer, we acknowledged his glance and I cried:

"Looks like a good one!"

Shortly, he asked our guide: "Want it for supper?"

Knowing that he doubtless was hankering for a taste of wild brook trout himself, I called out: "Save two or three. Never be better than when freshly caught."

The guide said to me, quietly, "I figured he'd be itching to wet a line. We have plenty of time to make camp before dinner."

"Better rig up and come on down," my son shouted. "There's another one!"

I was as eager as a kid to do just that but I had decided that one fisherman would have better luck than two. The inlet was narrow, the current strong in a comparatively short channel. The sun still was on the water. So I held back.

"Go ahead and fish. I have more chance to catch trout than you do."

Turning to the guide, I asked, "Trout in the Barrel Hole up at Fourth Lake yet?"

"No. It's been a funny summer so far. Anyhow, they don't ordinarily school there until mid-August or later."

(In comparatively shallow lakes like the one we were heading for—where the lodge was situated—Eastern brook trout seek cool, spring-fed areas when the water warms up appreciably. Thus, the term "Barrel Hole.")

The guide went on: "If we get a day or two of heavy rain while you're here, trout should congregate at the mouth of a brook, down-lake from the Hole."

The next day was clear and warm, so we elected to drive to a small, way-back-in pond—one I had not fished for many years and which, then, was reached by flying to a larger lake and hiking over a boulder-strewn trail to the little trout haven.

Now, our gear assembled, a lunch packed and strengthened by a hearty Maine breakfast, we boarded the four-wheel-drive unit kept at the lodge for just such expeditions. The first few miles were easy, for the road was well-kept by landowners and used for log-hauling. Then we came to a rutted lane. Wheel tracks went deep into muddy soil. Huge rocks stood in our way and we wondered how we would negotiate this stretch. Our guide assured us, "Only about a mile to the pond."

In low gear, he bounced the vehicle slowly up, over and around the rocks; rocked it out of muddy places. On its rack above our heads the aluminum canoe sighed and creaked, but its tie-downs held. We were jolted about. Yet the water came in sight and my memory pictured the fighting, deep-bellied trout that used to lie there below a small island in the pond.

"There were lily pads, I remember," I remarked. "You might think it was more suitable for bass or perch. The water was as cold as ice, though. The trout were hard to catch but abundant."

"Not too different than it used to be," the driver told us.

I sat on a canoe seat in the center of the twenty-foot craft, after it was launched. My son was in the bow and our guide paddled from the stern. Soon we were in the exact location I had recalled. As an anchor went down, trout began surfacing all around us. One jumped so close we might have touched him, had we been quick enough.

We were not long rigging our fly rods. Mine was a six-foot, 2¼-ounce English cane wand. My son's was a similar one of American make. Our early casts were made in full expectation of strikes but these failed to occur. After changing patterns repeatedly and casting tirelessly for an hour and more, I said:

"A famous writer friend of mine once wrote that anybody can catch brook trout, any time. I wish he were here now to show us how it's done so easily."

Sometimes we saw insects skating along on the surface. So we tried similar artificials, racing them by holding our rod tips high and skittering the feathers in imitation. I stayed with dry patterns. My son wondered if the trout breaking all around us might be feeding on hatches just below the surface. Perhaps their impetus as they drove upward was bringing them clear out of water in that nerve-wracking fashion. So he tried wet flies and then nymphs.

"It's not too different than it used to be. These fish are smart. If we held a net out one might jump into it! Doesn't appear we'll get any otherwise."

My son murmured agreement. The guide suggested we go ashore for lunch. Woodsman-like, he did not comment on our inability to get a strike, and when I offered my rod for a cast or two, he declined.

"Couldn't do any better."

On the way in, we slowed long enough to catch and return to the pond six-inchers that were lying in the shade beside the shoreline. They struck nearly every cast. The fly didn't matter. Any offering was accepted.

"When they live awhile, they certainly learn a lot of caution," my son said, laughing.

The guide told us a friend of mine had fished there the day before. "Nothing in the morning but later on he took five good ones on a No. 14 Doodlebug. Fished dry. It had a gray wool body and brown deer-hair, tied on lengthwise of the hook. He caught all of them on this one fly."

I had already cast a similar fly repeatedly but to no avail.

In the afternoon, I put on a No. 10 White Wulff and cast this big floater on the edge of the widening rings left by rising trout. After it settled for a minute or two, I would twitch it gently to bring it to life, then move it toward the canoe and repeat this procedure.

Half an hour passed and I stubbornly continued to cast the same way—a method that rarely failed me on numerous past occasions. All at once a trout took.

My rod tip swept toward the water. The singing reel was sweet music after so long a wait. Yet, when the brightly-colored lashing wild fish was brought to the canoe it looked small for this pond. I released it.

But now, with a bit more reason for optimism, we both cast frantically for the hours remaining that day. We were to meet our host back at the lodge for an early supper and I told our guide not to stay later than time allowed.

Only fifteen minutes more! A splash between us and the little island. A fish breaking. Then, only the dimpling circle where he had gone under again.

I laid the White Wulff on the edge of the ring, precisely as I had done with other casts all day. But now there was a savage hit. I shouted in excitement. "That's a good one!"

"Nice fish, Dad. Play him carefully!"

As I drew out the last quarter of an hour in superb satisfaction and, to a non-fisherman, incredible happiness, I heard an exclamation from the bow seat.

My son was fast to what turned out to be an identical brook trout.

"Man! If we could stay until dark, what action we'd have."

"You know something? Our host is flying in with the makings of a lobster, steamed clam and fresh corn dinner. He's probably mixing the martinis right now. Tomorrow is another day."

Still, we looked back at the little wilderness pond as we climbed into the four-wheel-drive and our mutual regard for this kind of place was strong.

We reached out and gripped hands. This time, I laid my other hand on my son's arm affectionately. It hardly seemed effusive.

10

SEVENTH QUALIFICATION:

Adaptability

During the Depression years, I learned that many men would rather starve or go on relief than change their occupations. If a tradesman was out of work, he was out of his own specific kind of work. He would not accept a job funded by the government, even when the routine tasks involved were minimal. He wasn't about to become one of those needed on PWA, WPA or whatever the alphabetical classification might be—maybe because of some of the jokes desperate wage-earners conceived in those dour days.

It took four men to cut grass, for instance: one coming, one going, one sh.t.ng and one mowing. The first thing built on a construction site was an outhouse, and government-sponsored employees with city residences didn't know that the boards which closed in the platform in front of the holes had to be laid up and down, not crosswise, to make the water follow the grain of the wood and drain down properly. So country lads took one peek at such a privy and parted the place for drier pastures.

It was a bad time but in some ways it could have been much worse. Note that common sense then dictated the immediate construction of an outhouse on every job. If there were more of these structures in Washington, politicians wouldn't feel compelled as they do now to unload on national television.

And if a man was out of work he had more leisure for fishing.

Later, when gasoline was rationed, only doctors and a few other professional men essential to our survival were given adequate gas for extended fishing trips, and the rest of us had to seek local species of gamefish and maybe depart from our confirmed fishing methods. Like the mechanics, many refused to do so: Once a fly fisherman always a fly fisherman, some avowed, ignoring the old adage that necessity is the mother of adaptability.

I decided catching salt-water pollock was a fair substitute for seeking salmon, since I couldn't get far away from my oceanside home anyhow. Except the time I was introduced to a man who really had it made. Not only was he a doctor but he doubled in brass as chairman of his town's gasoline ration board. He was compelled to drive several hundred miles every weekend to prove his quota was not overly generous. (Trips were, of course, reported as "business.")

Once, he asked me to fish for landlocked salmon at Maine's Sebago Lake, telephoning that he would pick me up and return me to my home with no sweat at all. We made the trip and I photographed him with a pair of fat, husky salmon and sent this picture to a Boston newspaper for which I did occasional free-lance work.

I gave the doctor's name and residence and the weight of the landlocks in my caption. However, one of the copy-desk men, thinking for some reason that the subject was a dentist, wrote this big, bold head, subsequently published: THE DOC SURES KNOWS HOW TO HAUL 'EM OUT.

The only thing was, Doc was not a dentist but an obstetrician.

The sea off the New England coast was heavily populated with pollock. So-called inshore fishing meant catches of smaller fish, known locally as harbor pollock to distinguish them from the big lunkers boated by commercially oriented anglers and sold to processers who marketed them as "boneless *codfish.*" (A lot of cod were filleted and salted and packed dry in wooden boxes, of course, but so were the misnamed pollock.)

It reminded me of a longtime popular fish in New England cookery—the scrod. Broiled, baked or stuffed scrod still is a gourmet's choice in many fine dining rooms, especially in Boston.

The scrod is any small inshore fish but most often a young cod nowadays, since haddock are scarce.

In Boston hotel restaurants and some of the other famous dining rooms, menu writers added an "h" to the name of this fish several years ago and the spelling persists there to this day. So, it's now sc*h*rod in many instances. (Perhaps some Puritan decided scrod was the past participle of screwed.)

Anyway, I pronounced the "h" one morning in the dining room of the Statler Hilton in Boston, where scrod or schrod is a breakfast choice. "Think I'll have an order of schrod," I told my waitress.

"I guess you don't come from Boston," she remarked. (I was born there.) "Here, we call it scrod."

"And in every dictionary I've checked 'scrod' is spelled without an 'h'," I rejoined.

"Well," she told me in all seriousness, "even Mr. Hilton can make a mistake."

Those piscators who failed to fish for other species than their noble trout and salmon in the time of the Depression missed a lot, however they spelled 'scrod.'

When pollock were schooling in early summer I used to row a small dory offshore a few hundred yards and tie up to a lobster-trap buoy. Then, rolling in the swells, I would cast a red-and-white bucktail downwind, give the line a yank and be fast to a scrappy gamefish of about two pounds. Just as quickly as that. Indeed, if the waves were high and my fly hit them on my back-cast, a pollock would seize it and give strong battle. Once I caught sixty pollock in succession, not missing on a single cast.

These small fish are soft. Good in a chowder if prepared the same day they're caught, they still do not match many other kinds of salt-water fish. I released most of the pollock I struck on those forays.

In recent years, fishing for striped bass in Massachusetts, New Hampshire and Maine, I often have hit into schools of pollock. In smooth-water harbors, these fish seem to lie deeper than those I caught in the swells but they still strike readily, fight hard and provide action when other gamesters are not taking.

In the Depression years and since, I cast a blue-and-white bucktail on a long-shank hook for a more edible species—mackerel. Or, troll for them with multiple-fly rigs on a spreader. They are scrappy and when two or more hit a trolled rig simultaneously a fisherman has his hands full.

When we were limited in our driving, too, I learned to appreciate a gamefish that was and still is abundant in New England: the white perch. Known as "the poor man's trout" in Maine, this species is so heavily populated in many lakes and rivers that it can be taken without limit during the open season. (That includes scores of ice-fishing locations and thus almost year-long angling for white perch is legal in Maine.) The white perch is closely related to the striped bass, but average size and weight are much less than we associate with the stripers, of course.

The perch is landlocked now in Maine but was originally a migrant from the sea. Not to be mistaken for the yellow perch, the white perch is similar in coloration to the largemouth black bass in the cool waters of Maine, at least. In spring, families fish for perch from bridges over small rivers and in inlets and outlets of lakes. They use worms on small hooks. (A No. 5 trout-bait hook is about right.) Usually you use a sinker to take the bait down and a bobber on the line to show when a perch hits. A rod may be fly-, spinning- or alder-pole.

White perch will sometimes hit a small fly. A good time for that is from daybreak to sunrise on smooth water. They also hit small spoons, bait and spinner rigs and other lures. Evening, too, can be productive.

Occasionally one catches them when trolling for other gamefishes but, more often, they are taken by still-fishing with worm-baited barbs.

The size and weight of white perch varies from one body of water to another. A six-year-old may be a foot in length and weigh more than a pound in one location and be less than seven inches and weigh only a few ounces in other ponds. The world's record was established in 1949 when a white perch of four pounds, twelve ounces was caught in Maine's Belgrade Lakes region. Perch of a couple of pounds are not too uncommon but, where populations are especially heavy, pound perch and under are the rule.

The poor man's trout can be filleted and dipped in batter for frying. The meat makes a tasty chowder, too. These fish are bony, and the larger white perch are, of course, easier to skin and fillet.

In recalling white-perch fishing trips, an incident can be included that lightened an otherwise uneventful day for me and a friend. We had started out by trolling a popular central Maine lake for landlocked salmon but, when we failed to get a solitary strike, we anchored our sixteen-foot boat over a re-membered perch hole and soon were boating some good ones.

By Maine standards there was considerable traffic on the lake that day. One big inboard craft came close enough for us to hear the conversation of the obvious owner—a much overweight character who was sprawled in a fishing chair drinking beer and fondling a pretty girl while his guide held the wheel and looked over his shoulder occasionally to catch any salmon strikes. They were rigged with heavy deep-troll-ing rods and lead lines that we knew carried long strings of spinners and sewed-on baits.

Just as they came directly opposite our anchored boat, the guide shouted, "You've got a hit! Rod on the port side. Rod on the left—your right."

"Well," the owner's voice ordered, in a highly nasty, unpleasant tone, "haul it in. What the hell do you think I'm paying you for?"

"That," said my companion, "is what's the matter with the sport of fishing today. Like everything else, it's been ruined by wealth and authority."

Meanwhile, the guide had idled his motor and was busily reeling in the hardware. There seemed to be a mile of it. Then he gave a sharp yank on the rod butt and into their cruiser came a white perch about six inches long.

The swinging hooked fish arced directly at the "sportsman" and, intentionally or not, the guide wrapped the perch around his boss's neck. As the big-bellied owner dumped his girl friend on deck and clawed at the fish, the guide kept slapping his bloated red face with the perch.

We doubled up laughing.

"That guide won't be working tomorrow," my friend decided. "But I'll bet he doesn't give a damn."

11

EIGHT QUALIFICATION:

Jocularity

Some fishing trips are so anticlimactic that a sense of humor is a requirement to keep friendships on what sailors call a level keel.

One such expedition was conceived during a deer-hunting trip a few falls ago. Three companions—a public relations director for a large woodlands concern, a game biologist and a consultant working out of the state university—planted the germ in my mind and then, during a break in an annual meeting of Trout Unlimited, fertilized the growing plant of anticipation to a point where we set a date for a wilderness jaunt to northern Maine.

The pond we were to fish for brook trout that "run up to four pounds, maybe more" was inaccessible except by four-wheel-drive vehicles. There were no fishing lodges on its shores, so we would tent out. We would need to haul in our own canoes. And if we hit the fishing on the nose as we expected to, we would find our ice refrigerators to be indispensable containers for keeping limits cool and firm on the way home again.

I wondered why my PR friend packed steaks, bacon, eggs, beans, potatoes, ready-mix flour for biscuits and bread, all kinds of pastries and pudding mixes.

"If the trout are so plentiful, seems like corn meal, a piece of salt pork and a dozen cartons of beer would be all we'd need for a long weekend," I suggested. There were sickly smiles that disappeared as one of the boys reminded me that the PR rep loved to cook.

We drove a heavily loaded car and the four-wheel-drive unit over miles of logging roads and finally arrived at a log camp on Caucomagomac Lake late one Sunday afternoon in June. The black flies were so thick that we decided against tenting on the remote pond, which lies some distance from Caucomagomac. We unloaded our supplies at the camp and soon had our first meal of hot biscuits, steak and potatoes (and even a tossed salad) topped off with slabs of homemade apple pie, cheese and coffee.

Next morning, not bright but early, we put our tackle, fly spray, some sandwiches (sandwiches? What about eating trout? Where's the frypan?) and four cartons of beer in the winch-equipped vehicle, along with rain-gear, always an essential in Maine, and then hoisted two aluminum canoes on a pipe rack overhead, with poles and paddles lashed to the canoes.

We jounced and bounced for hours over seemingly impassable, grass-grown, mucky, rutted byways, frequently hitting hidden boulders for diversion and stopping to axe-cut blow-down trees that lay across the road at intervals.

Our game-biologist friend had driven all kinds of vehicles in Korea, "often at night, without lights," he recalled, "so this is nothing. Don't worry, we'll make it okay."

When we arrived at Wadleigh Stream, the crossing was a

rock-strewn ford and we decided to unload the canoes and push them over—*if* the Jeep could make it all right.

It did, but not until we had pushed and hauled and pried it off a huge rock, where it had hung precariously on the driver's first fording attempt. He backed up and rammed it ahead once more. It stopped on the opposite bank and we waded over and shoveled down the steep pitch so that, on the next try, the unit finally stood steaming and cooling opposite three men and two canoes. Now we pushed these over, reloaded them and were ready to continue on to the magical trout haven our maps indicated lay but a few miles distant.

The canoes fell off the rack once in a while. We were wet from Wadleigh water and sweat outside and slightly damp from beer inwardly. We slapped black flies, swore, climbed in and out of the vehicle as occasion required and, ultimately, arrived at a point where the pond lay like the proverbial sparkling jewel in the sunshine that filtered down through richly green firs and spruces.

Now, we told ourselves, we would soon be fast to fabulous fish and forget our arduous efforts to get here.

We shouldered the canoes to lakeside, loaded them with essential tackle and beer—plus a plentiful supply of fly dope—and soon pushed off to try our luck. There was a tent on the first point. There were five canoes on the small pond, each with two or three anglers aboard. A bush pilot's plane took off as we began casting flies. Another circled and swept down, its pontoons making waves that rocked our canoes before those from the other pilot's takeoff had subsided.

"Looks like we have competition," I remarked to my kindly PR pal, who deserved the label of kindliness, since he was paddling while I fished.

He sighed. "Maine's not like it used to be."

I was thinking how much easier it would have been to have flown in, since that appeared to be customary. The planes really were active—unloading a trio of fishermen and helping three others climb in to replace them. The shuttle service would have done credit to as busy an airport as O'Hare in Chicago, I decided.

Yet the sunshine was warm and companionship was pleasant. Anglers don't talk much and this was just as well, since we couldn't be heard over the planes and outboards, anyhow. I cast until my arm ached, ultimately thinking, "When I start changing flies every five minutes, I know the action is slow, to say the least."

At noon we met for lunch and to talk over what the battle plan would be next. I had hooked and released one small trout and our friends in the second canoe had not done much better.

The biologist went up to the Jeep and shortly came down to lakeside with a small outboard motor, canoe bracket, deep trolling rod and a can of worms. He soon took two or three bait fish and threaded one onto the barb that was tied to his heavy leader ahead of a huge metal spoon. As he and his buddy of the morning shoved off again, he announced: "We're going to troll. If there are any big trout in this pond, they'll be lying near bottom. Sun's too bright for fly fishing."

I told my PR paddler, "They used to have a saying in New Hampshire, when I lived there years ago, that fitted occasions like this: 'The futility today is like trying to put a pane of glass in a cat's ass without any putty.' "

He wasn't giving up yet and he insisted on continuing to paddle while I fly-fished another section of the water, including an inlet stream. But if there were brook trout anywhere, I couldn't catch them.

After a futile hour or two we returned to the main lake and, spotting our pals, we approached to see how they were doing. The biologist held up a big togue (lake trout) and shouted: "Nine pounds."

Just then they caught another fish of nearly the same weight.

Then, they motored over and suggested that we try out their rig, since the two lakers they had taken gave each his legal limit of seven and a half pounds apiece plus.

I remarked that I hadn't trolled for togue for many years but would try anything to break the spell we were under that day.

My buddy insisted again on letting me fish while he ran the motor. Our friends lifted their two lake trout out of the canoe and lowered them in a big net into shallow water, to keep them fresh. We passed over the places where they had hit togue and then ran up-pond a short distance. There was deep water under my tackle and I fed out additional line. Just then the rod bowed and the line fed off more quickly. I let the fish mouth the bait and then struck him hard.

"Got one! If I don't lose him."

I reeled and reeled, grinding away on the handle. Finally, the laker dipped and dove and struggled within my view.

"Get the net. He's coming in."

My buddy held up a little brook trout net, laughing wildly. "They took their big net to hold their fish! This thing isn't big enough for a twelve-incher. What'll we do?"

"Run the canoe ashore," I said. "When we get into shallow water I'll step out and lift him in by the gills."

We towed the togue several hundred yards. The wind had begun to blow, waves were running high now and the canoe took the swells sidewise, splashing us thoroughly.

When the bow beached it rested against a steep bank of sand. I asked my pal to hold the rod while I stepped over the side. First foot touched bottom but the waves washed over the top of my rubber-soled boots, filling them both as I gingerly felt my way toward the land.

I caught hold of the leader and dragged the togue toward me, then reached down to free the hook and grab him under the gills. More water ran into the top of my pants, but I gave the heavy togue a toss up on the bank and would have climbed up after him except he slipped back and now thrashed around weakly beside my boots. I stepped down hard on the fish, ran both hands under the cold water and this time was able to close my fingers under his gills and give him a heave into the canoe.

We were laughing so hard we almost swamped the canoe as I climbed aboard once more.

"Boy! You certainly are an ethical angler. Wow! Stomp 'em into submission. That's how you do it, huh?"

We had a pool for the heaviest and second heaviest fish caught. My togue was second. When we dressed it later, however, about a quart of water washed out of it and the boot marks were on the side where we had towed and stepped on it.

I told my friends: "This should get me kicked out of Trout Unlimited, The Federation of Fly Fishermen and a few other ethical associations, unless you fellows keep that togue under your hats. If all of the ambitious clubs I belong to should realize their goals, I'd be up to my thighs in turkeys, up to my dingle in ducks, up to my groin in grouse, up to my tonsils in trout, up to my feelers in dry flies, up to my dongle in deer and up to my ass in bass. They all want to bring back wildlife and fish populations until we're wallowing in them. I salute them all and only hope that none of them finds out how I caught that boot-marked, half-drowned togue today. That's all."

My pals reminded me that, in The Making of an Angler, a sportsman should experience all kinds of fishing methods, so he will learn to appreciate the fine art of fly-casting.

I said, "Yeah. When I think back to my boyhood vacations on the Maine seacoast and remember tying a handline to my big bare toe and trolling that way with a clam-baited hook for pollock, mackerel and anything else that happened along, perhaps stepping on a togue is some sort of a refinement after all. But we had to row our boats in those good old days and a big toe was like another finger."

12

NINTH QUALIFICATION:

Selectivity

When an angler has learned many practices and thinks that he has achieved considerable skill and professionalism, incidents occur that cause him to realize perfection is still a distant goal.

For example, once when I was fishing for brown trout in a small lake not far from the ocean, I noticed flocks of seagulls diving and feeding excitedly. They were half a mile from where I was casting flies and, since action was slow, I decided I would experiment by following the gulls, as many knowledgeable salt-water anglers are prone to do.

While motoring toward them, I recalled a rather extraordinary conversation I had engaged in on an extremely cold January day the winter before, while driving through Portland with a resident of that Maine city. Noticing that his windshield was cracked, I asked him how it had happened.

"A big seagull flew over the car on one of those 25-below-zero mornings we've been having and as I glanced up through the window he let go a big splash of white crap. It froze on the way down, hit my windshield and made that crack," he explained.

I laughed heartily, but he frowned and I saw that he was, indeed, not kidding. I had watched gulls so many times picking up frozen mussels, clams and other bivalves from the flats at low tide and then hovering and wheeling over a bridge or highway to drop them on a hard surface in order to crack them open. Then, as it seemed certain to me my friend also must have noticed, the gulls would sweep down, alight and pick away at the choice morsels so ingeniously freed from the shells. Occasionally, a rock or piece of frozen mud would be dropped by the feeding gulls and when it hit the road from a considerable height it would bounce like a golf ball.

"It must have been a rock that hit your windshield," I persisted. "As cold as it's been here, excretion wouldn't have time to freeze hard enough to crack the thick glass in a car."

"It was crap," he expostulated. "I tell you I saw it expelled and watched it freeze in the air!"

I laughed again and asked: "Did you file an insurance claim?"

"Damned right. And I used the common four-letter word in my report, too. Don't want any city adjuster to get fouled up in his thinking. Some of them are dumber than a native New Englander," he concluded, staring at me coldly.

I couldn't help chuckling, no matter how angry he became. I could picture the employees of a large New York insurance company reporting drowsily for work on a Monday morning: nobody smiling; most of them unhappy to begin another Blue Monday, telling themselves, "Three hours to lunch time and a couple of Bloody Marys. How can I stand it?"

Then a weary secretary opens the claim letter and starts to scream with laughter. Her boss grips his hung-over temples and stares at her apprehensively. Has she finally blown her top?

"Oh, no! Listen to this! A man in Portland, Maine . . ." More laughter. He gets her a container of coffee and frowns.

She swallows and starts again: "A man in Portland, Maine, files a claim for a broken windshield. It was so cold that when a seagull flew over his car and crapped, the stuff froze solid, fell like a rocket and smashed his glass. Oh, my Lord. I've got to go to the lady's room."

As she rushes away from her desk there's a small streak of moisture trailing behind her. The claims adjuster picks up the letter and calls everybody together. He reads it aloud. The staff breaks up. Their president comes in to see what the hell is going on and he has Xerox copies made for the next insurance convention.

"Like, we think we have it tough in New York City!" he shouts, slapping his leg and laughing.

Back on the Maine lake in June, as I closed the gap between my boat and the feeding gulls, I picked up a pair of field glasses and studied the wheeling birds. They appeared to be feeding on smelts. Well, that should mean brown trout chasing the little bait-fish, and a streamer fly that looks like a smelt should interest the brownies, I decided.

In the education of any angler, there comes a time when he knows enough not only to make simple decisions like that but to have confidence in those decisions. But I think maybe the time never comes when every decision can be guaranteed to produce. Each decision has several consequences. First, obviously, it leads you to select a particular fly or other lure. Then the refinements come, in a chain of further selections— whether and where to cast or troll your offering, how to present it, how deep to fish it, and so on. Even a gull, who spends his whole life practicing, misses an occasional smelt. Even a gull can mistake a rock for a clam, or fail to break a mussel on the first few drops. Even a gull would have to get damned lucky to crap and crack a windshield on every try. About all you can do is make what you think are the best possible selections in a given situation and back them up with contingent selections.

In this case, as the gulls continued to dive and feed, I tied on a Black Ghost fly while my boat drifted in among the birds. The smelts were breaking water over a wide section of the lake. I cast the Black Ghost as I circled the outside edge of the smelt school, dropping the streamer right into the silvery splashes. Once or twice I saw brown trout arc their backs as they came up, chased the food fish and then dove under the surface again. They were driving me crazy. I didn't get a strike.

Then I tried trolling streamers as I continued to circle the outside of the smelt school, zigzagging so my fly would work erratically among the smelts. No soap.

I recalled fishing in the evening for brook trout on a northern Maine pond under somewhat similar conditions. I had seen bait-fish breaking—being driven and fed on by large squaretails, it seemed certain. So, as I was doing here while fishing for browns, I had begun by casting streamers for those speckled trout and hadn't had any hits, either. A guide had suggested:

"Pick up your dry-fly rig and cast a No. 4 or 6 Royal Wulff right where those smelts are surfacing. Let the fly float for a second, then give it a twitch as if it were trying to escape."

I thought, "Anything is better than what I've been doing."

My first cast and twitch of the dry pattern brought a savage strike from a two-pound brookie, I remembered. Then, following the school around until dark, the guide gave me some of the fastest, most exciting action I ever enjoyed.

Why hadn't I thought of casting a dry fly on that other occasion? Wasn't I supposed to be achieving some skill and selectivity myself? Or did I have such a long way to go in the making of an angler?

As I reached for my dry-fly rod that day on the pond, thinking maybe I could reenact the scene that jogged my memory, I laid my wet-fly rig beside me without having yet reeled in the streamer. It drifted and sank much deeper than I'd been casting, I suppose. Anyhow, now ready to try my dry fly, I started to reel in the Black Ghost when, BANG! A brownie hit so hard he nearly yanked the rod from my listless fingers.

I gave line quickly. The rod bowed, the reel sang, my pulse

rate jumped. The brown trout sounded. Then he came up and out like a salmon, shaking off water like a retriever dog. Man! He was a good one.

In a little while I had him alongside. This was a five-pounder, as I subsequently found out, and I kept him to prove to my family that when I said I was going fishing, why, that's what I did.

Was this the single silly brownie in a school? Or, should I fish deeper, more slowly, with that Ghost fly? It happened on that occasion, at least, that the streamer was the brown-trout medicine, when I allowed it to sink and then reeled it in fairly fast. (I wonder how often a fisherman selects the right tactic by sheer accident and then, when the memory begins to blur around the edges, almost convinces himself he did it by sheer cunning.)

I told myself that experiences like this are what makes fishing such diverting sport and, above all else, such experiences humble a person who has begun to think he knows it all. Only a gull could catch one every time—or almost every time. Only a gull has such deadly aim from both ends, too.

No wonder the old gray-haired salt-water fisherman came up with that wisecrack to bring a governor down to earth. It had happened years ago, when I first started doing promotion for Maine. Land had been given on oceanside for a state park, and the governor and key legislators were visiting the area with the donor to look over the gift. I was assigned to take pictures of the sand beach and of the dignitaries—naturally. We found our way to the principal section of land barred by a swiftly eddying tidal river. The ancient mariner was there with a tiny skiff to ferry us across, one at a time. As everybody drew back, hesitating to climb aboard and risk his life in the crossing, the old fisherman hollered:

"Jump in, Governor. We elect one of you fellows every few years. Easiest man in the crowd to replace, you are."

A true Mainer himself and a war hero, the gubernatorial incumbent laughed and took the maiden passage.

He was first in on our return trip, too.

13

ON THE IMPORTANCE OF A

Refresher Course

In the making of an accomplished angler, I have found that I need to return to fundamental practices occasionally, if I'm to display the skill that helps me perform the more intricate casts and modestly show off a considerable ability to excite gamefishes to strike my offerings when I'm acting out my role before an audience.

This is important. Without the appreciation of others, a fisherman's life loses a lot of its meaning. He is somewhat like an actor but in or on a watery stage, and his plaudits may be nothing more than winning the pot for the largest fish; or the chance remark: "Man, are you lucky." (Said enviously, of course.)

So, one should not fail to go fishing regardless of what kind of action is anticipated, or what sort of tackle is used. For one never knows the tricks he may learn anew, or how well they may apply to angling in loftier locales with more sophisticated equipment.

More things happen to me when I am fishing than when I am dreaming about it. And even the humblest excursion for picayune panfish may bring unexpected opportunities to exercise one's expertise on more glorious game.

It's like the field mouse who was wandering about one summer's day, as male field mice will, in search of amorous adventure. Having encountered no female field mice, he was about to turn homeward when he chanced on a gigantic cow moose. The cow was holding a front hoof in the air and grimacing in pain. Asking what ailed her, the little mouse was told by the great moose, "I've got a big thorn in my leg and I can't get it out."

The rambling rodent seized the splinter in his tiny teeth and jerked it free. The cow sighed in relief.

"Anything I can do to reciprocate?" queried the mild-mannered moose. "I am a fine specimen in the largest of the North American deer family," she reminded the little mouse, "and I like to return favors of this kind."

"Well," the small creature squeaked, "it may amuse you but I've always nurtured a notion of making nooky with a great big female like you, Miss Moosey."

"Go to it," the cow said, agreeably.

So the mouse ran up the moose's hind leg and began his lovemaking.

Just then, a dead limb of considerable dimension fell from a large white oak tree and banged down on the cow's neck. She grunted and the mouse called out in sympathy:

"Am I hurting you, dear?"

Now, sitting around home and watching TV, who would ever have an opportunity of seeing a wildlife drama like the foregoing? (Come to think of it, the way things are going nowadays, I expect we might catch a clinical class in child sex education showing something similar to negate the birds-and-bees business we were brought up on.)

Anyhow, hardhearted anglers know full well that a live mouse makes a highly acceptable bass bait. I prefer the artificials, personally. A ʹnobler end for mice is in a cancer-research laboratory. It's all a matter of opinion and even prejudices. Right?

If one wants the whiskers from a bull moose for bucktail flies—as an aside—one might do well not to pull the beard of a live bull from mid-August through early fall in the north-woods country. That's when these mammals are mating; or, specifically, when the bulls are in the rut. Their disdain—maybe antagonism—for stream-wading anglers during that period should cause a fisherman to pause and contemplate the effects of palmated antlers pushed against his posterior precipitously. Personally, if I see a bull moose I get the hell out of there.

A second aside: Teddy Roosevelt is said to have conceived his Moose Party split while he was at camp in the Seven Ponds section of Maine. To this day, one of the log cabins contains a mounted moosehead of impressive size (believed to be the very bull Roosevelt gazed at, while he was on a fishing trip in the Megantic Club holdings). The club is still active, in an area of Maine that is the headwaters of the famous Kennebago Lakes and the Rangeleys, where President Herbert Hoover once took a large Eastern brook trout on a streamer fly. This is the wilderness, too, through which Benedict Arnold and his rag-tag Colonial troops passed in great pain and suffering as they inched their arduous way to try to capture Quebec City, far to the north of Megantic.

Thus does an angler acquire quiz-show information.

Nevertheless, the theme of this chapter is pertinent to practicing fishing itself and renewing skills and knowledge from prosaic pastimes in order to perfect oneself as a professional piscator.

Consider how catching salt-water smelts through the ice of a Maine river or bay can improve techniques for trouting. Both species have small, tender mouths and if they are struck hard by over-eager anglers, then the barbs of baited hooks or flies pull out and away goes the quarry.

I see myself seated on an upturned nail keg in a stove-warmed smelt shanty on a brackish, tidewater river that is frozen sufficiently (I hope!) to support not only my rented shanty but a hundred others of similar design and layout. Before me, a long trench has been cut through the ice and another similar opening is on the opposite side of the shanty. From a cross pole are a succession of drop lines, equipped with sinkers and with small hooks that are baited with little pieces of sandworms. From time to time I reach up and jiggle the pole and this moves the baited hooks beneath my feet.

If there is a slight movement of the lines to left, right, ahead or back under the ice, it can mean feeding smelts. (These fish run from six inches up to eight and ten inches or more. They are a highly sought-after species, delicious when fried in butter and crumbs.) And fishing for them is great fun, too.

The action may be fast when the tide is running in—for an hour or so before high tide—and when it is ebbing for another hour or more, since the smelts follow the current upstream and then drop back with it later. There are literally thousands of them at times and action can be fast and furious, so much so that two men are needed to tend the lines on either side of the shanty when this occurs. (Often three or four fish from the same shanty.)

There are dull, fishless periods, too. As in all fishing, I might not hit a good run for several days—or nights, since a lot of the fishing is on night tides. Then again, schools of the silvery smelts can keep me occupied in an incredibly wild feeding spree.

The tide draws the lines under the ice. Any materials in the current may snag the lines and cause them to move erratically, too. So it takes sharp eyes and training to distinguish between real strikes and other movements.

If there is any doubt, or when one is certain that smelts are hitting, the fingers close quickly but gently on the drop line and the line is pulled in steadily, without a final jerk until the swimming smelt is seen in the murky water below. Then, a steady but quick toss lands the smelt on the ice, where it is picked up and put into a container with—one hopes—other smelts being kept for that fine feed.

So it is, one learns, when striking a trout on a fly: There must be a gentle uplift of the rod tip to hook the fish and then careful, steady retrieving of the line—never allowing slack to occur but not keeping the line so taut that the hook pulls out of the trout's tender mouth, either.

More skill is required to be a mouse than a moose, when fishing for most species, then, but emphatically so when the contest is with salt-water smelts or the historically noble trout. This I learn by fishing—as you do, too—not by armchair dreaming.

Now smelts usually are hooked so lightly that they fall off the barb when iced. Trout may have the hook deeper in the lip, occasionally even inside the mouth. If they have swallowed the hook they might as well be kept for the frypan but this happens infrequently and I have found that one way to release them without rubbing away the protective coating of slime that trout wear is to simply hold the hook by its shank quite firmly and allow the wiggling fish to shake itself free. This is no trick at all when barbless hooks are used in fly fishing and when small dry flies are cast with barbs. Few trout die if properly released.

Sometimes Mainers take a frypan, some grease and corn meal along on smelt-fishing trips. With a thermos of coffee and a lemon to squeeze on the cooked smelts, those who catch the migrating smelts and cook up a feed on the spot really have a taste to remember. The shanties have a small stove for heat, so there's a ready cooking surface. (There are even electric lights with power from a generator in the smelt shanties I rent on Maine's Eastern River between Augusta and Wiscasset. And bait, lines, etc., all are included in the deal.)

I have to get used to the sound of groaning ice as the tides rise and fall and to look at the long, deep cracks in the frozen surface and tell myself there is little danger. Don't the owners of the shanties drive their trucks right out on the river, after all? Walking and sliding out a few hundred yards from shore and returning to my car after fishing is over, nevertheless, I shudder a bit and am happy to feel the firm snow-covered earth underfoot again.

Yet it is well worth the small effort and slight apprehension to experience the excitement of tidewater smelting in midwinter when the open-water fishing season seems far ahead in Maine.

This is so different from ice-fishing on the lakes inland from the seacoast. Yet that, too, is sport and that, too, helps me to retain some small habits so consequential in the making of an all-around angler.

14

Diversification

There are a few kinds of gamefishes that are so cooperative they will strike any offering—even when crudely presented. Thus, an angler may learn the use of fishing tackle a step at a time, matriculating from one school of angling to another, continuing his piscatorial education indefinitely if he wishes to do so, with a single fish.

In Maine, that species is the chain pickerel. It is one of four most abundant fishes in the state. At one time pickerel were caught commercially in Washington County, Maine, and sold on the Boston market and elsewhere. Even as this book is being written, there is no size or weight limit on chain pickerel in that county—where they still may be sold— although elsewhere in Maine a limit of ten pickerel has been established.

Pickerel are caught by anglers nearly year-long across the

80

state, since they are a favored prey of ice-fishermen. A warm-water species, they populate lakes and streams from the center of Maine south to the seacoast for the most part, with an occasional stretch of water slightly farther north containing these popular gamefish.

Because of the enthusiasm for trout, salmon and bass in Maine, pickerel often are overlooked by anglers. A few are caught incidentally while sportsmen are fishing for bass and, again, ice-fishermen do seek pickerel as a principal species from the time ice forms in the fall until the limited open season on salmon and trout begins February 1.

Those who "discover" Maine chain pickerel in the sections where they attain weights of two to six pounds, and occasionally more, have many exciting sessions fishing for this species.

When I was a young man I often joined congenial companions pickerel fishing in southern New Hampshire, and later continued this activity occasionally after moving to Maine. My initial experience catching chain pickerel in the Granite State was with a long cane pole, purchased for ten cents in an old-time general store. These bamboo sticks might be twelve and fifteen feet in length.

I found that my instructors would tie a piece of strong white twine to the tip of the pole and wind more of it around and around the end until several yards of line were stored there. The end of the string was tied to a long-shank, snelled bait hook. No weight was added. The bait usually was a chunky strip of home-cured salt pork.

Standing in rubber boots in shallow, weed-grown water, or fishing from a wide-beamed rowboat, the angler swept the long pole in an arc and "hove" the pork strip into the water lilies and pickerel weeds. Then he twitched it back toward his stand or boat, bouncing it noisily, then allowing it to rest, then giving it another quick jerk and stopping the pork strip momentarily once more.

In familiar pickerel grounds savage lunges by these predaceous fish occurred with satisfying regularity. Sometimes they would take the bait the minute it hit the water; it rarely escaped their attention for more than a couple of those noisy jerks that were accomplished by practiced "skitterers," as anglers who fished this way were then known.

The fisherman let the pickerel mouth the pork rind, despite the speed of the murderous strike, and after a minute or two he would snap the rod upward and drive the hook home. A real battle ensued. Sometimes the fish would tangle line and itself in the strongly rooted weeds; or perhaps the fish would dive under a sunken log or rock and sulk there. It was more often strong-armed into the air and flung back into the bushes. Then the angler dropped his long pole and trotted ashore (or rowed his boat in, as the case might be) to grasp the long, toothy snout in back of the eyes and above those viciously sharp teeth, in order to free the hook and add the pickerel to his bag.

Lying in shallow water, pickerel can be seen as they make that incredibly swift lunge for food. In sunshiny, hot early summer days, they appear to be active, contrary to trout and salmon. They feed on perch, frogs, water snakes, ducklings, small song birds, mice and immature muskrats—to mention a few items in their varied diet. They will take every kind of artifical lure, including streamer flies. The worm fisherman can catch them, too.

In Maine it is unlawful to use for bait in inland waters any pickerel, goldfish, yellow or white perch, bass, sunfish, crappie, hornpout, carp or any spiny-finned fish, but smelts and mummichogs can be and often are offered to pickerel and other gamefishes. Years ago a popular pickerel bait was a strip cut from a perch belly, but the Maine law now reads that prohibited baitfishes cannot be fished dead or alive, so this offering is out for the law-abiding angler.

I graduated from the long cane pole to a five-ounce fly rod and from pork strip to big bucktails and feathered streamer flies. Pickerel will cut through nylon leaders with those sharp teeth but I still find a six-pound leader will usually suffice to bring in a few of these gamefish. Some anglers prefer to use light wire leaders and they are more practical, of course.

Flies take savage beatings, too, so my own preference is a

strongly-tied bucktail on a long-shank hook—about size 2 and 4. Mickey Finn, Red and White, others are good.

From the early skittering days, I continue to skitter and bounce a fly when pickerel fishing, and the method is effective for me. Sometimes I can see the fish start off with the captured fly and I try to delay striking for a fraction of a second—hardly as long as when the offering was pork rind or live bait but sensing the wild surge of a pickerel, his mouth open hungrily, then, just as he turns away with the bucktail lightly mouthed, I hit back at him and usually hook him firmly.

Thus does continual practice at fishing, whatever the species—in fresh water or in salt—keep one's reactions timed, one's senses attuned, so that an angler in the making is in physical condition and possessed of mental alertness sufficient to maintain his standing with his piscatorial pals, it seems to me.

Besides, it's a lot of fun—not only fishing but listening to guides tell their stories. Like this one, for instance, related to me by a pickereling guide:

"I was working one summer with another guide and we were showing two couples from Boston where to fish in this section," he began.

"It was a dry, hot summer. The other guide weighed two hundred and fifty pounds. He was built solidly but his belly looked like a display of retread tires. He hated the sight of water and refused to take a bath, let alone a swim in a lake. In the kind of weather we were having, he sweated and smelled like a dead bear. Naturally, the wives complained to their husbands and the husbands bellyached to me. I told my fellow guide he simply had to take a soaping down and a dip in the lake or get through. No way out of it for him."

The guide laughed, remembering. He continued:

"That evening we were camped out on an island. I persuaded my buddy to follow me to the far side, well away from our sports' tenting ground. I took towels, soap and a body brush, because I knew this was going to be a man-sized job. I had a pint of rotgut liquor as a pacifier. Nobody was going to get that woodsman to take a swim unless he got him half drunk beforehand."

He laughed again.

"Well, I poured the booze into him, pleaded and begged until he undressed. Then I took him by his big paw and steered him out into shallow water. He looked like a bear just out of hibernation and, like I say, he smelled worse.

"The way he lifted his feet and put them down again, you'd have thought the water was either boiling hot or ice cold. It wasn't either, of course. Finally, he was in up to his knees and I began to soap his back, neck and ears. Then, I handed him the soap. It slipped from his fingers and fell into the lake by his feet. He stooped over to pick up the bar of soap and, do you know, as he straightened up again, a peck or more of beechnuts tumbled out of the fatty creases in his big belly.

"We hadn't had a crop of beechnuts in this country for ten years," our guide concluded. "That'll give you some idea how long it had been since he had a bath."

I was pickerel fishing on that occasion with a friend from New Hampshire. (We had lived for several years in the same small town.) Not to be outdone by our guide, I asked my friend: "Remember how straitlaced the girls used to be in that New Hampshire seacoast village?"

He nodded.

"Years ago, when the men used to bunch up hay on the salt marshes back of the ocean, they had a term for the haystacks. They called them haycocks, remember?"

He nodded again.

"Well, there was this maiden lady who was so prim she wouldn't say manure if she stepped in it. I won't tell you her name because I don't want to soil her reputation."

He laughed.

"Anyhow, her old bachelor brother was bunching up that salt swale one late summer afternoon. They used to feed the marsh grass to livestock to make the animals thirsty so they'd drink a lot of water and grow faster.

"The lady had a visit from a cattle dealer and he inquired for her brother.

" 'Wal,' she told him, 'Jake is down in what they call the Gila Swamp, *a-doodlin'* up the hay'."

The story would have gone over better if a big pickerel hadn't hit his fly precisely at the punch line.

15

ELEVENTH QUALIFICATION:

Exploration

There's something about far places that intrigues anglers. I remember when I lived in New Hampshire that I rarely stepped into a brook from the highway to begin fishing but, instead, cut across the woods to reach a location without a beaten path on the stream bank. Later, I followed local sportsmen or guides to farther away places, seeking always, as is customary with anglers in the making, virgin water to fish in.

When stocking of gamefishes assumed importance, fishermen perhaps caught more trout near a road; for the hatchery trucks dumped adult brookies in such places, of course. In ye good old days, trout fingerlings were backpacked in cans to headwaters and planted there, with the supposition that they would grow naturally and migrate downstream to mingle with the native fish. There was appreciable loss from

predation and, anyhow, sportsmen demanded heavier stocking of legal-sized trout. Hence, the highways adjacent to brooks and rivers were used increasingly by hatchery crews.

In sportsmen's associations it was considered unethical to follow a tankload of fish and begin casting while the trout were dumped into the water. Still, some practical anglers ignored criticism and many took home quick limits on opening day. These fish were known as "liver-fed" by those who refused to angle for them and who, instead, still continued to seek out remote pools away-back-in.

Then, with the advent of small planes equipped with pontoons, fingerlings again were airlifted and stocked through ingenious tanks from barely safe flying heights by daring pilot-wardens. Mountaintop ponds received quotas of brook trout in this way. Some of these were too small for planes to land on and fishermen had to reach them by climbing wilderness trails or even by following maps and compasses through dense woodlands.

There was added spice to adventuring of this kind, and these far places attracted the more serious anglers. Now, even some of these waters have been depleted and bush pilots wing over uncharted forests to reach still more remote waters in Canada. Many outdoor writers, realizing that their nationally published articles reveal "secret" sanctuaries even so distant in modern times, vow never again to specifically describe how to get there.

One man remembers his story about a northern Maine pond, reached years ago by small plane, where Eastern brook trout weighing two to four pounds were caught just after ice-out in the spring. "I ruined the fishing with that one article. Hordes descended on the little pond and the big trout breeders were soon hauled away. Stocked fish never since have had time to attain the weight of those truly native brookies."

Once, years ago, I could be assured of taking enough trout for supper in any one of thousands of Maine wilderness ponds and lakes. It was simply a matter of being there in early evening, placing a dry fly in a logical spot and knowing how to hook a striking fish correctly. Indeed, as hatches occurred, rising trout by the hundreds would suck in mayflies, leaving a widening ring to indicate to a caster where they were lying. Some would leap clear of the water, too. A floating fly, dropped in or near that ring, would result in a quick take and an exciting battle.

It was a rare occasion when another fisherman was on the same piece of water—unless he was with me on the trip. Indeed, if we spotted a canoe on a wilderness lake, as we prepared to land our plane, we would wing to another pond so we could fish there alone. Things have changed in a few years, with planes now shuttling anglers to what were "unspoiled" waters a quarter of a century ago.

It seems to me that the popularity of trout and salmon (and black bass) contributes largely to the growing scarcity of these species in certain places. Thus, I am seeking to show sportsmen in this book that fun can be had catching anything from eels, hornpout, pickerel and perch to the rarer brookie, brown, rainbow, landlock and coho.

I remember the comment of a commercial fisherman after his initial experience trolling a Maine lake for landlocked salmon. A friend of his had enticed him to go there. Used to hauling in several hundred pounds of ground-fish (cod, haddock, pollock, etc.) and harpooning an occasional bluefin tuna of 500 pounds and more, this lake fishing struck him as a highly foolish pastime.

"We pulled little flies behind a boat all day long," he chuckled, "to catch two three-pound landlocked salmon apiece. My buddy told me we were lucky. Almost caught our limit, he said. Those salmon would be culls where I fish at sea. They weren't any bigger than an inshore scrod!"

So fishing can be a matter of preference and certainly an attitude of mind. Indeed, it well may be that the tougher it is to catch a trout, bass or salmon, the greater the challenge and therefore the keener the pleasure when one does score.

Besides the allure of far-off waters, there is the magnetism that draws one to the abodes of exotic species of gamefish. Once abundant in many Maine lakes, for example, the rare blueback trout became nearly extinct in recent years. It still is found in a few waters, and fisheries management personnel in the state have stocked bluebacks in some experimental locations to preserve the pure strain of this species. Believed by some scientists, at least, to be a landlocked kind of Arctic Char, the blueback, I found, is hardly an exciting fish to catch, but it did prove not too easy a prey until a pilot-guide let me in on a secret of his.

We had flown in and landed on a small pond near the Allagash section of the state. It was early summer and I tried wet, streamer and then dry flies, which took a few small brook trout but failed to interest the bluebacks.

I wanted bluebacks to photograph. I wished more to satisfy the excitement and pull of an unusual species in a remote location, I suppose.

Finally, my guide told me that if I didn't mind using a tiny red-and-white spoon, bounced off the bottom as he allowed his canoe to wind-drift the pond, I could take the bluebacks. He handed me one and it was so small I had no difficulty using it to replace my fly.

As I changed lures, he paddled upwind. I fed off line until the spoon hit bottom and then lifted and dropped my rod tip repeatedly, as he suggested.

Soon I felt a tap and then brought a blueback of about eight inches to net. Then, another one took the little spoon. Shortly I had boated half a dozen bluebacks and had satisfied my urge to explore this kind of action in a far-away location.

Once more I was impressed with the value of experience that gives guides the knowledge of how, when and where to fish, especially when they are in their own localities. Other sportsmen had told me that dry flies would be effective at the time of year I would be trying for bluebacks, but without the suggestion from my guide on that occasion I would have made the long trip fruitlessly.

Not only that, but I would not have heard another of those stories going the rounds in the northwoods.

"You've met that big old-timer on Eagle Lake—the one who hunts bears and bobcats with hounds," my guide began.

I nodded.

"And you know his close friend from Fort Kent on the Canadian boundary?"

I nodded again.

"Well, they like to play jokes on each other, as you doubtless remember. The latest was a beauty. Seems the bear hunter is very fond of strong cheese and his pal takes some out to him from Fort Kent every time he calls at Eagle Lake. One evening recently he got some cheese that was so strong he had to wrap it in several layers of aluminum foil and drive to the bear hunter's cabin with his car windows open all the way.

"When he pushed open the cabin door and stepped inside, the old man was sitting in front of a roaring fire and his favorite old bear and cat hound was lying in a doze at his feet. 'Brought you out some more cheese,' he told the old hunter casually.

"As the old man unwrapped several folds of aluminum he remarked, 'Notice you did.'

"He broke off a corner of that odoriferous cheese and dropped it down for the hound," my guide told me, smiling.

"The dog sniffed, took a bite, then dropped the cheese and curled around and began licking his rear end.

" 'Man! That sure is strong cheese,' the cat-hunter exclaimed. 'Look at that hound trying to get the taste out of his mouth!' "

I laughed. "Reminds me of the first time I ever met that big old hunter," I rejoined.

"I'd flown north with a game warden-pilot when I was working for the state. We had the Governor aboard. A world-famous war hero and highly regarded citizen, and he was a great human being besides.

"That old hunter knew very well who he was but when he came out to his landing to help anchor the plane, he shouted in that bull-moose voice:

" 'Hi, there!' to the pilot. 'How the hell are you? And, who the hell is that bald-headed old so-and-so you've got with you?'

"The Governor roared. 'You and I are going to get along just fine,' he told the woodsman. Then he stepped the rest of the way onto the landing dock, grasped the old-timer in a bear hug and told him:

" 'Reminds me of the clergyman who used the word eunuch in one of his sermons. After the service, this young chick asked him what a eunuch was and he told her it was a bald-headed man. He was as bald as a billiard ball himself, and the girl said, 'Then you must be a eunuch.'

" 'No,' he replied, 'I'm two-balled, Miss.' "

The blueback guide said, "We could use some of that kind of humor in government nowadays."

I nodded. "That Governor really enjoyed the out-of-doors life. He was up there for a fishing trip. The old bear hunter was a good fishing guide, too, remember?"

"Sure was," my guide agreed. "As a matter of fact, it was him first showed me how to catch these bluebacks with a little red-and-white spoon fished off the bottom."

16

Plain Luck

While my chief goal has been to acquire skill in taking trout and salmon on a dry fly, the greatest thrills have come from catching—or even watching others catch—giant gamefishes of the sea. Considerable know-how is required by both a boat captain and a sportsman in persuading mammoth fish to take a lure and then in fighting the quarry to gaff. And I believe that, perhaps more than in freshwater angling, luck is an essential element in ocean fishing, too.

Once, when I was involved in promotion for the State of Maine, I was contacted by a nationally known writer who was living in southern New England at the time. He told me by telephone that he wanted to come up, go out on a bluefin tuna boat, catch a tuna and return home the same day. He asked if I would take pictures of the action, so he could spend a few hours making notes for an article he had been assigned to write for the then prestigious *Saturday Evening Post*.

I was flabbergasted. I told him that most of the bluefins taken in Maine were harpooned, but he said, "No," he must get a tuna on rod and reel.

I reminded him that our state-sponsored tuna tournament had proved so chancy that we were on the verge of discontinuing it. The first year, forty-two bluefins had been caught by rod-and-reelers and we had been highly pleased with the resultant publicity. After the initial surge, however, the annual take by sport fishermen had been any given number from a top of six or eight to a low of zero.

"And this was during a week-long tourney, not for a few hours in a single day!"

He asked and I said, "Yes, there are large schools of tuna offshore, especially out of Bailey Island in Casco Bay. But fishing with rod and reel, for only a few hours—"

The free-lancer assured me he would take a chance. He would meet me in Brunswick and ride from there to Bailey Island with me, next morning. I promised to call him back.

It wasn't easy getting a boat captain and mate on short notice, especially men whose boat had a fighting chair in the stern. Harpooners, yes; sport-fishermen, no, not tomorrow. "Call me next week."

I finally located two commercial fishermen who had added a chair to their lobster boat. This craft was old. We later named it "The Mackerel Cove Whizzer," since it used Mackerel Cove, Bailey Island, as home port.

When I met the writer in Brunswick next day, we stopped at a local restaurant for coffee and I had sandwiches made up for our lunch. My new acquaintance was a slightly built man and I thought that, if he were to hook a tuna, the fish would haul him overboard. He was quiet and modest. His car was of ancient vintage. My first impression of the whole deal was that this was going to prove worse than I had anticipated.

I asked him if he were an ardent angler. He said no, that he kept busy writing. I noticed that he had an old folding

Kodak camera on a faded neck strap and wondered how he expected to take pictures of acceptable quality for the *Saturday Evening Post.*

On the ride down to the island our conversation was anything but inspired. He didn't make any notes, so I gave up trying to inform him about tuna fishing in Maine.

The two men were waiting for us at the landing and both of them smiled as they, too, sized up the situation.

Once we were underway, nevertheless, the writer did take a small notebook from his pocket and he asked the captain and mate a few questions over the noise of the motor.

In a little while we were over the fishing grounds. They baited a big hook, strapped the journalist in the chair and showed him how to feed off line, how to lift the rod tip occasionally to jiggle the bait and how to alternately reel in and pump the rod if a bluefin struck.

"Ain't more than one chance in a thousand that a tuna will hit that sewed-on mackerel," the captain observed. "We couldn't get any better bait but don't make much difference. Only sensible way to catch tuna is to harpoon them. Sometimes they'll hit a drifted bait and some of these charter-boat crews nail a stray fish trolling, like we are. Most are harpooned, though."

His mate was in the platform built out over the bow, searching the sea for surfacing bluefins. Suddenly, he pointed his finger in an easterly direction and shouted to the captain to "run her over there. Fish showing!"

As we slowed down at the edge of a school of breaking fish, I saw a big fin cleave the water; then another one cut a wake as something chased the smaller fish. I pointed but the captain and mate already were aware that tuna were active and I knew they were hungering for their harpoon.

We heard a shout and, looking astern, saw that the writer was into a bluefin. The mate leaped back toward the fighting chair and began to bellow loud, profane instructions, but the writer was doing everything as calmly and correctly as if he battled tuna regularly for a living.

The sea was reasonably calm. I took picture after picture

of the action. The writer kept on churning the big reel handle and in a surprisingly brief time he had the wire leader showing. The two men worked together, one holding the leader while the other gaffed the tuna. They hauled it aboard.

The writer smiled quietly. The captain swore. "One of the smallest bluefins I ever saw out here. It'll weigh fifty or sixty pounds at the most. Well, let's try for another one!"

The writer now told us that he was satisfied. He'd had the experience of catching a tuna and, if a bigger one were to strike, he felt a huskier man should be in the chair.

So the captain quickly took over as the mate sewed on a fresh mackerel for bait. The mate took the wheel and began circling the area where school fish still might be seen breaking water. I moved back of the fisherman, camera ready for a quick picture-taking session, if we were lucky enough to tie into another bluefin. The captain pumped the rod, excited now, and obviously cheered by the unbelievably fast action on that first fish. I looked at my watch and saw that we had been out only a couple of hours.

The writer climbed up on top of the cabin roof and sat there with his short legs dangling. He snapped a few pictures from that vantage point and I thought it was too bad he didn't have a modern camera, for the angle would show the captain in the chair, the boat from center to stern and the gulls wheeling over the low waves of our wake. I knew I was too heavy to test the cabin roof for similar photographs but decided, "What the heck? I have enough anyhow. Plenty of action on the writer's fish. Too bad it was so small. Looked more like a dolphin than a bluefin."

To everybody's surprise, I'm certain, the captain suddenly shouted, "I've got a big one on! Slow down that engine! Circle him! I need all the help from the boat I can get!"

There was a steady stream of profanity now between the captain and mate. (Anybody who has heard the colorful obscenities and blasphemous language of irreverent Maine coast fishermen will know what I mean when I say that even an atheist will shiver apprehensively as the air turns deep purple from their oaths. Those who swear bring new words

and phrases into our language. Others, like my great grandfather, who always carried a Bible in his pocket and who
prayed frequently and passionately, are extremists in the opposite direction.)

It was a long battle this time, for the bluefin's power was
apparent, despite the relentless pressure on the rod clutched
in the huge, hairy paws of the captain and the skillful handling of the wheel so the boat favored the fisherman every
inch of the way. I recalled incidents like this, with tuna boats
being out for six and eight hours and even then with the
bluefins tireless and anglers exhausted. Only the hook pulling free, the line snapping, or the fisherman cutting the line
and quitting to preserve his own life had terminated some of
those battles.

But the energy of this monster was matched by the
strength of the captain and the experience of his mate. The
line began to come in steadily now, and when the first of the
leader showed the captain shouted:

"Harpoon him. This is the biggest tuna I've ever known.
He'll set a world's record. Go over a thousand pounds!"
Then he caught a glimpse of the fish in the water: "Maybe
1,200 pounds or more! Drive that harpoon into him, quick!"

The mate did as he was told. When the iron point struck
that tuna, he came out of water like a jumping salmon. Gal-
lons of the salty sea washed into the boat, as the fish smashed
the surface, sidewise. I pivoted to save the camera lens and
was soaked instantly from neck to feet.

The harpoon lay on the water, for the iron had not penetrated the thick hide of the bluefin. The mate hauled it in for another toss but it was too late. When the giant body had fallen back into the ocean, it had landed on the leader and line and snapped it like it was a piece of thread.

Then the cursing really gained tempo. Each of the men blamed the other. Both profanely called on the saints to witness the stupidity of his companion. I retreated into the wheel house. The journalist still sat calmly on his perch. He had folded up his camera now and was busily writing notes in his little brown book.

Those were the only tuna of that day. The men spent another hour or two searching the sea but to no avail.

On the way back to the cove, the visiting writer interviewed the captain and his mate, quieting them down with his own placid mannerisms. My respect for him went up notch after notch, particularly when, on our return drive from Bailey Island to Brunswick he described some of his experiences as a war correspondent and as author of official books on most branches of our own armed forces and those of several of our allies.

I told him I did occasional free-lancing but, at that time, I still received rejection slips occasionally.

"Began writing in high school," he murmured, rather apologetically, it seemed to me, "and so far I've never had a manuscript turned down."

This was as incredible as his fishing luck. We both knew that he had to be one of the luckiest men alive to have hooked and boated a fish just equal to his own strength and to have watched what might truly have been a world-record tuna, all within a few hours' time.

I still wondered what his article would be like and even if it would be published. But, when he mailed a copy to me within a surprisingly short space of time, I found it to be completely factual, gripping with excitement, and as interpretive of the Maine scene as anyting I had ever read.

He thanked me for the many pictures I had taken and told me in a letter that they had helped to refresh his memory of our adventurous trip. However, the one photograph used as a "double-truck" spread over his story title, "Bluefins are Bedlam," was a highly dramatic shot of that huge tuna in the air beside the boat stern, water spraying, men tensed, rod bowed, harpoon flung—the works—which he had taken, of course, from his precarious perch on the cabin roof, while I, assigned to cover the trip, was half drowned from the wash of fish-flung waves. That was a humbling education for me, both as a writer-photographer and as a so-called "authority" on fishing.

I recall another occasion when I visited an inland area in late May with newsmen and famous sports personalities. We had the baseball players in for trouting and ourselves for wire-service stories and pictures. On that occasion my pictures were used nationwide.

However, what I remember most was a remark by one of the many daughters of the couple who ran the fishing lodge where we were housed for a long weekend. This camp was reached by flying in from Portage Lake in Aroostook County, Maine. The daughters were in camp for the Memorial holiday period and, as several of us newsmen and baseball players were being shown to cabins, we went past a log cabin with open door and windows, for it was warm and sunshiny there.

The daughters were chatting away, as girls do. One of them said, in a clearly audible voice:

"Mum and Dad told me to get in here and help out. What's going on? How come we're open so early in the year?"

We stopped to eavesdrop.

"Don't you know?" Another voice. "Professional ballplayers and a lot of writers are arriving for the weekend."

"Geez," the inquisitive girl observed, "Guess we won't do any bare-assed swimming in the lake this time, huh?"

We laughed. The kids looked out the window, saw us and drew back. The one who made the funny remark waited on table and during subsequent meals we couldn't get her to say a word except "Yes" and "No." She was truly embarrassed—

a genuinely modest country girl. We felt sorry for her, and some of the ballplayers autographed baseballs for her personally.

But, as we boarded the plane after the weekend was over, one of our crowd shouted back:

"Now you can go in swimming, girls. Hope the water is warmer than it looks."

17

Of Small Significance

Smallmouth bass do not have little mouths, as fish go; only compared to largemouth bass are the jaws a bit less gaping. So it is natural, I suppose, for anglers to assume both kinds of bass prefer to gobble down big live baits and to hit sizable plugs, spoons, spinners and poppers, rather than to accept insects and small artificials.

A few years ago I decided this assumption could be erroneous. At least, on certain occasions.

My son was camping with his family on the shore of a western Maine lake and he spent considerable time fishing for smallmouths there. One evening he called me and said that if I would come over he would demonstrate a new bit of bassing technique. His secret proved to be catching husky bass on tiny No. 16 dry flies. Fishing for them precisely as anybody casts on evening hatches for trout—indeed, match-

ing the insect hatch as to size and general shape and color—
he convinced me of the efficacy of this method.

Using a two-ounce fly rod, No. 5 forward-taper line and a
leader tapered down to 3X, he struck smallmouths consistently. Others, using plugs and large baits, did not.

He brought to net a three-pounder, lost another good bass
when his leader broke. Hits by one- and two-pound fish were
so frequent the effectiveness of "trouting" for bass was con-
clusively proved, so far as I was concerned. Since then, I
have made occasional trips to bass waters with only my light-
est fly-fishing tackle along.

As in casting dry patterns for other gamefishes, my luck
has been best in mid-season and during evening hours, when
natural hatches were occurring. Spring or fall bassing still
means (to me) wet lines, big streamers and popping bugs, or
bait-casting and spin-casting of plugs, spoons and spinners.
Live baits and bottom-fished worms are normally productive
at any time of year. But, again, my son's demonstration left
me believing that on certain occasions nothing would produce like a little dry fly.

On a typical August afternoon this year I paddled a small
canoe across a bass lake in central Maine. The light wind was
dying. Insects were buzzing. Swallows were picking bugs off
the surface everywhere. In a sheltered cove, pickerel weeds
and white pond lilies grew profusely. Old stumps and an occasional boulder showed where smallmouths might lie. In
spots, tree limbs heavy with green leaves provided shade
some distance out from shore.

My hands trembled as I rigged my light rod. I fitted a No.
6 line through the guides and bent on a tapered leader with
terminal strength of four pounds. For I knew these bass
would burst from the weed beds, if they hit; then in wild
frenzy, when they felt the barb, they would lunge back into
their cover of tough-stemmed lilies.

My fly was a No. 14 Mosquito. I false-cast, then dropped it
at the edge of the weeds. It lay there looking natural to my
prejudiced eyes. Apparently a bass agreed.

There was a surge as if somebody had fired an underwater

rocket toward my canoe. My first thought: "A pickerel! It'll break the leader."

But the fish came up directly under the little fly, snapped it into its lip and protested that I was in for trouble if I thought for a second I was going to outwit it. I could feel the jolt of the strike and the immediate battle for supremacy in my right arm and somewhere deep inside myself. The mind of a fisherman?

I put all of the strain I dared on the bass. It came out of water like a high-diver does following his plunge. Shaking water, its head vibrating to free the fly, its tail now arcing so the black, glistening body was a vibrant bow, it smashed the surface with the noise of a flung stone.

"The weeds! Keep it out of those weeds!"

As I thought these warning words, my second thought was that light-test tippet. It would hold, I knew, if handled carefully in open water. But, those weeds?

Once the smallmouth did reach his shelter. I pulled steadily and as firmly as I dared under the circumstances and managed to bring him back into the safety zone.

Repeatedly he jumped, shook and dove. His runs still were long and strong. "For its size, there's nothing more powerful than a bass!" I whispered.

Just when I thought he had tired and even as I was steering him toward my net, he made a final run and was into the pickerel weeds.

I moved the canoe closer and looked down into his haven. The leader was wrapped around the tough stems, sure enough. I pushed my net under the bass—for it, too, was snarled close to a particularly large weed. With a yank upward, I brought bass, weed-tops and all aboard.

The hook had been freed by the net bow. I lifted the smallmouth out by its lower jaw, held it up and guessed its weight at three and a half, maybe four pounds. Then I lowered it back into the lake. Not regretfully, either. This one deserved its freedom; that much was certain.

My net was a mess. Several strands were broken and wet weeds clung to it in clusters. I spent a few minutes shaking and picking it clean again and decided it would do.

When I examined the fly I was puzzled how it had held. The barb and bend were straightened as if by a metal tool. I discarded it and tested my leader for strength, then added a new No. 14 Mosquito to its apparently safe tippet.

Moving down beside the weeds a paddle stroke or two, I cast again. Once more, a bass smashed the fly. Always amazed that any gamefish can see such small offerings, I was reprimanded mentally for my inattention and remaining disbelief in the acceptability of tiny dries for such big-jawed antagonists. This one was in the weeds before I could turn him. The leader parted. I knew the fish would rub the fly loose on bottom gravel, so I wasn't concerned for the bass, only for my slow reactions.

When a third cast a short distance below brought the third jolting hit in succession on the same pattern—tied to a new leader—I decided this was going to be one of those great evenings. This time I brought a two-pounder canoe-side and released it, after a tingling touch-and-go contest.

For two hours that remained before darkness drove me ashore, I hooked and fought smallmouth bass. One or two pickerel smacked the tiny fly and tangled my leader before breaking free. I caught yellow perch and sunfish, too. But the action was largely with husky, vigorous, unyielding bass. My arm was lame before I quit.

I would be back tomorrow, I vowed. But the wind blew night and day for a week thereafter. It rained hard most of the following week. Things came up that needed my attention at home. By the time I could go bassing again, fall had arrived and the offerings were quite different from No. 14 dry flies.

So, an angler dreams of seasons to come: each requiring different practices to attract gamefishes, and each, notwithstanding, offering superb sport. That is, when fish are taking like those smallmouth bass on that August evening, with conditions just right and a heavy hatch in progress.

18

THIRTEENTH QUALIFICATION:

Superstition

Few life-long anglers admit openly to their superstitions but those who live so close to nature do nevertheless come to accept as gospel the basically unfounded beliefs that have been handed down from their ancestors—who, in turn, acquired such notions from their own progenitors, as well as from the Indians and, oftentimes, from seafaring men who brought back from distant ports weird beliefs and odd customs.

Even in my earliest angling days, then, I would not think of using a thirteen-foot cane pole. If it happened to be that length, I would cut off a few inches before venturing on a fishing foray.

Friday the 13th was a day to stay in camp; not one to occupy with piscatorial pursuits. Indeed, a fly tied on that date not only would fall apart but probably would be driven into a finger or cheek by a capricious wind.

Once, as a small boy, I was spending my annual summer vacation with my maternal grandparents in Kennebunkport, Maine. (My parents were living in Boston then, so I was taken to the North Station of the Boston & Maine Railroad and placed in the care of a conductor. He promised to remind me to leave the coach at what was then known as "Upper" Kennebunk and transfer to a local train that would discharge me at "The Port." From that station, I would walk to my relatives' home on "The Crick"—a small harbor making inland from the open sea.)

Sailing and fishing nearly every day with my grandfather, I only experienced seasickness once. On that occasion I anchored a skiff in the center of the creek and fished all day in bright sunshine for flounders. I had a drop-line with a sinker and small hook, baited with pieces of clam. The fish came well and the day passed so pleasantly that I only rowed ashore when the tide ebbed so low I had to leave.

The water was glassy smooth but I expect that I became ill from too long exposure to sun glinting off the surface and beating down on my bare head. Anyway, I took my fish to my grandparents and then climbed into a bunk my father had built, when he converted an old barn into an abode for our Maine summers.

When I failed to appear at the homestead for supper they came looking for me. My body was burning with fever. I was dizzy, faint and mostly unaware of my surroundings.

My great grandparents lived in half of the house my grandparents occupied. The old lady was known then as an "herb" doctor and many local residents would summon her to sick beds before they would call a professional practitioner. She felt my forehead and, turning to my grandmother (who had been christened Adliza Grant Smith), she said, "Ad, go up back of the woodshed and pull off half a dozen big burdock leaves."

When she had these in hand she lifted my shirt and laid several on my chest and abdomen; then she placed others on my forehead.

"Always place the leaves with the point down—toward the

feet," she emphasized. "That way, they draw the fever from the body and expel it through the extremities."

They told me afterwards that she changed the cool leaves several times in the night but I was unaware of anything, as I fell into a deep sleep and awakened next day "as fresh as a daisy," as the old-time saying went.

I grew up firmly convinced of the factual nature of such assertions as: "Hardwood should always be cut on the full of the moon in the fall, stored until late winter, then split on another full moon. The heat from burning it is much greater than from wood cut any old time."

"Green apples will cause *cholera infantum* and *cholera morbus.*" (Intestinal diseases that used to occur in summer.)

"Children should be seen and not heard." (This was a strict rule at mealtime. My great grandfather often told me that his twelve brothers and sisters and he were fed at a long shelf, standing. "We learned that eating while standing would help our food to run down easily," he remembered.)

The old folks were exceedingly temperate but they made elderberry and dandelion wine and drank it in the spring for a medicinal tonic. They had brandy in the house in case of heart attacks. From sailing days, too, they knew the efficacy of hot buttered rum to ward off or cure colds. Social drinking was out, except for a small glass of wine offered to visiting neighbors, if they were so inclined.

Once, as I grew older, I sat in a fish-house talking with a commercial fisherman. He had had a rough weekend, partying with friends, for his habits differed from those of my grandparents. I knew he was dying for a drink and suggested that we go up to the old house, where we would enact a bit of dramatic persiflage.

"With any luck, maybe we can help that hangover," I told him. He agreed anything was worth a try.

So, just as we climbed the steps on a side porch, he fell down and lay there moaning. I rushed to the door, moved inside, and shouted:

"Quick, Granny! Man's had a heart attack! Get the brandy."

Before she caught on to our deviltry, she had run outside and, kneeling, poured the raw liquor into his mouth. He seized the bottle from her gnarled fingers and dumped a great swallow down his throat.

She took the bottle back and drove us off the porch with a broomstick.

That fisherman was a firm friend of mine for life. Times without number he took me in his old lobster boat and, with his traps hauled and crustaceans sold to a dealer, he pointed the nose of his dory to secret fishing grounds where we caught big sea cunners, flounders, rock cod, harbor pollock, mackerel and, of course, the inevitable dogfish. Always, we would recall the time my great grandmother saved his life with a slug of brandy.

My ancestry in that part of Maine goes back to the earliest settlements by Welsh, English and French immigrants. They lacked transportation, like colonists in most sections of New England, so marriages were pretty much restricted to a small area and, while actual incest doubtless was rare, they sometimes wed second and third cousins, if not first cousins.

I was quite young when I first played doctor with some of the little girl cousins, then, and my grandmother, who had a suspicious mind, informed me sternly that she knew what we had been up to.

"How do you know that?" I demanded.

"A little bird told me," she replied.

So I saved my pennies and bought a slingshot and later an air rifle and took pot shots at every bird within range. I didn't hit any, but I tried. That's all I can report about my doctoring ability then, too.

When a maturing child is frustrated to this degree he naturally will put more emphasis on his fishing. Or, become a dedicated bird-watcher in later life.

In the making of an angler, superstitions that are impressed strongly on the mind when young do cling like entangling vines all through life. Walking down a trail to a fishing stream or lake, if the person ahead goes around one side of a tree, I follow. I wouldn't dream of taking the opposite side, even if the path were smoother there.

I do not walk under a ladder. Maybe nothing will happen, but why not be sure?

I don't sit down to a table with twelve others. I may look foolish but I'm not that mad!

I do make some concessions. If I cut myself on a fish knife, I let a doctor give me a shot of penicillin. (It's difficult to find an old barn-loft that is dusty with cobwebs, nowadays, even though we always used cobwebs to stop bleeding in the older times.)

Thinking about bucktail flies: Hair from the tail may be okay but I've been led to believe the belly hair from a buck is hollow and hence it floats better. So, I ask my supplier where the hair came from when I'm buying a new lot, and, knowing me, he asserts: "It's genuine buck belly."

Once I complained that some of his materials looked moth-eaten. "Had it here all winter?"

He opened the door with one hand and, carrying a few feathers in his other fist, he stepped outside, then came right back inside.

"Just came in," he told me. "Couldn't be fresher."

There are many superstitions that anglers are aware of; for

instance, when the green leaves on hardwood trees turn upside down in the wind, anybody knows it's a sign of rain. (Maybe not today but soon, anyhow.)

When New England weather is fine, with sunshine and cloudless skies, an angler doesn't need a prophet to remind him that the day is a weather-breeder—meaning torrential rains and maybe hurricane-force winds to follow. It's a wonder one has the courage to venture out on a river or lake, so many things can occur.

If there has been an extended spell of fine weather and the fish are slow to strike, a sudden thundershower will wake them up. While it isn't safe to cast with a rod in hand during the lightning flashes, as soon as the storm ends that's the time to be there.

If it has rained for a week and the sun comes out from behind scattering clouds, fish should show interest, too.

How many of these convictions are superstition and how many are factual is something for the individual angler to decide.

I have seen them work either way, myself.

19

FOURTEENTH QUALIFICATION:

Susceptibility

Perhaps my own humble beginnings had an effect on my later susceptibility to those who have worked so that I might play at becoming an angler. I always have felt more at home with guides and sporting-lodge operators, with boatmen, small-plane pilots and farmers than with individuals possessed of prestigious positions and six-figure salaries.

Anyhow, I am attuned to the humorous yarns told by woodsmen, and some of the more amusing ones are recounted by French-Canadian fishing guides as we sit around an evening campfire on wilderness canoe trips in northern Maine. Their accent adds greatly to these anecdotes, and writing them detracts from the stories in vocal form. The French-Canadians put emphasis on certain syllables in their speech and I'll italicize parts of words for this reason.

Their jokes always begin modestly and follow a pattern sometimes called, "a short story with a long tail." Typical is

the one about an old trapper named Louis, who was hob-
bling around a tiny hamlet with his leg in a plaster cast. His
friend Francois asked him how he broke his leg and he
answered:

"Last winter I was on my trap*line* and one afternoon it
started to snow hard. It was cold, maybe twenty below the
broken-bulb ass-end of the thermometer. What you think? I
don' know. She was making ice in the trees, any*how*. They
was cracking and groaning like a virgin bearing twins. How
that done? You don' go to church? No wonder you don'
know nothin'.

"I was freezing my water-*pump,* an' if I hadn't bumped
into Pierre's ca*bin* real quick, I don' know what I done.
Pierre, he was in town, his wife tol' me. But she said, 'Come
in. Come in. You'll freeze your beech*nuts* out there.'

"Then she made hot tea, gave me a drink, I think she
saved my life, Francois.

"It was too cold to leave. She gave me another drink,
cooked some deer *meat* and tol' me, 'Get in Pierre's bunk.
He don' come home tonight. When he goes in town he gets
drunk. You know Pierre.' "

Which reminded Louis of his own dry throat and he
steered Francois into a beer joint before continuing with the
rest of his tale about how he broke his leg.

Quaffing beer and sighing, he went on:

"I am one big damn fool, Francois. How I broke my leg
you ain't going to believe! When I get in Pierre's bunk I am
tired, dead-tired, Francois. That woman ask me, 'Anything
else I can do for you, Louis?'

"I tell her no.

"Twice in the night she wake me up and ask, 'Anything I
can do for you, Louis?'

"In the morning, too, after she cook big breakfast—salt
pork, beans, eggs, hot biscuits and lotsa cof*fee*—she put her
hand on my leg and she say, 'You sure nothing else I can do
for you, Louis? You real sure?'

" 'No. Nothing. You done plenty, already. You good wife.
Pierre lucky man.'

"She rubbed my leg and tell me: 'I'm woman enough for

more than Pierre, Louis. Anything else I can do for you?' I tell her no again.

"Then I pull on my heavy clothes and say Goodbye and finish my trap*line.*

"Last week, spring is coming, ice is breaking up, Francois. My cabin roof is leaking and I get a ladder and some new cedar shakes and I'm on that roof fixing that leak. That warm sun she thaws out my water *pump* and something makes me think of Pierre's wife. How she kept asking me if she could do anything else for me.

"I tell myself, 'Louis, you big damn fool!' because I know now what she offer me. I get so damned mad I kick myself in the ass, fall off the damn roof and break my leg."

Another one concerns the French-Canadian farmer who lost his prize bull. A neighbor asked what happened to his bull and he explained it this way:

"That damn man on the draw-*bridge,* he don't know a bull's ass from a steam*boat.* My bull she take sick. I call that man what is the *vet*-erin-*arian*—how you say him?—and he tell me the bull she have *con*stipa*tion,* what you call a sore throat in the ass, ain't crap for three week.

"He tell me get a fun*nel,* mix up a pail of soap *suds* and pour the suds in the bull's ass.

"I do and the bull she get mad, break out of her stall and run down the road. When she come to the draw-*bridge* that bull is toot-tooting through the fun*nel* and that damn tender, he open the draw and my bull she fall in the ri*ver* and drown.

"That draw-*bridge* tender, he run for that job once more and I vote to replace *him.* He don' know the differ*ence* between a bull's ass and a boat whis*tle!*"

I was reminded of how the old Yankee New Englanders put such short stories with long tails into a few crisp words. When a well-known politician addressed a large audience, for example, and I asked a fishing-guide friend what he thought of the hour-long speech, he replied:

"Went over my head like a blast of gas in a gust of wind. Or a bean-caused boom in a blizzard."

And the old-time traveling medicine men had a different

cure for constipation in man or beast than the northwoods vet. They prescribed a live grasshopper swallowed backwards. When it hit bottom it would kick the crap out of a patient, they explained.

Which brings me to the selection of a few fly patterns for Maine trout fishing. In dries, the Grasshopper in sizes 10 and 12 is effective and I have hit big brook trout when fishing evening hatches by casting a No. 8 and even larger sizes. Casts are made, the fly allowed to drift lightly on the surface; then the rod tip is given a twitch to jump the Grasshopper and BANG! a brookie takes it—if he is at all interested on that particular occasion.

The Grasshopper also is a good pattern during daytime fishing on trout ponds, especially if there is a little wind to kick up the surface.

The Light Cahill in similar sizes is particularly appealing to Eastern brook trout in northern Maine waters. So is the Wulff series: Brown, White, Royal and Gray. There is a local pattern called The Kennebago Wulff that is obtainable in Maine's Rangeley region, where the famous dry-fly Kennebago waters (Little, Big and Kennebago River) are located.

Originally tied on Maine's Sandy River north of Farmington to entice hits from brown trout there, a popular fly across the state for brook trout, too, is the Cooper's Bug, Doodle Bug and in some places still known as The Devil Bug (although wrongly, since, I have found, this is a registered trade name for a bass lure known as Tuttle's Devil Bug, long in existence and still in production at last account). The Cooper's Bug, said to have been conceived by a John Cooper of New Hampshire when the Sandy River browns were only hitting something similar there, is a true fly. Its body may be fluorescent—green, black, brown, red or some other color. The wing is simply tied from the hollow belly hair of a deer (for flotation) and the hair is laid lengthwise on a hook, in sizes from 8 to 12 for brook trout; 12 to 20 for browns. Both ends are cropped off.

I long have been surprised that this pattern is not more widely known. It is in just about all Maine tackle stores and fly-tying shops. A fly-fisherman in that state would as soon leave his rod at home as to be without a few of these flies. I wrote a *Field & Stream* article on the pattern years ago and had hundreds of letters from anglers the world over, who reported great success with it, especially when cast for brown trout.

I have taken brook trout on it both from the surface and by using a sinking flyline to take it down. Once, I cast it as a nymph in September and caught a limit of bottom-feeding brook trout that had failed to take any other offering of mine on that occasion.

Browns in the pound- to two-pound class take it well in spring, when terrestrial insects are falling from tree limbs that overhang the water's edge. Then, sizes 16 and 18, cast right in under the trees and floated there for somewhat longer periods than if I were fishing for brookies, are especially appealing to browns. Again, a slight movement of the fly, after it has lain quiet awhile, brings a savage strike from these gamefish.

Such dry-fly fishing for Maine brown trout is done on smooth water. When winds blow I cast a brown bucktail with red tag and white-tip tail, allowing it to sink to bottom, lie there for a time, and then to be brought up for successive casts. Our browns take offerings much more slowly than our brook trout do.

There are many other choices of flies for Maine trout. At the start of the season, when water and air are cool, if streamer flies fail to produce (not often) then I find that olive-green nymphs in 12 and 14 sizes can be what they are looking for. I cast them on a wet line, sink them to bottom and then move them at well-spaced intervals. The hits come on or close to bottom at such times.

When I write the words "brook trout" I am usually considering the wild and stocked speckled Eastern brook trout—not merely any trout found in brooks. Much of our fishing in Maine is in small lakes, which we know as "ponds." Another local name for this "brook" trout is the squaretail. The fish is probably the most popular species in Maine. Browns are far fewer in number and in fewer waters, too.

To prove how whimsical trout can be, I usually follow a rule from experience of casting larger floating flies during the evening rises. However, while out with three friends in two canoes on a recent summer trip, I saw that they were getting follow-ups and jump-overs by sizable brook trout at a piece of water known as Big Island Pond. I had a two-ounce cane rod rigged and it was too light for big sizes like they were using. So I tied on a pattern in size 16—a fly that had been stashed away in my kit for years. An almost forgotten pattern, too. A Red Ibis. The trout went wild over it.

They were tricky to hook that evening but I had action galore for once while my friends went fishless.

When they asked the name of the dry fly and I told them, one of the younger anglers said:

"Red Ibis. Never heard of that pattern."

20

Some Questions of Preference

A reader inclined toward what has come to be known as "ethical" angling (fly-casting to the exclusion of all other methods of fishing) will, perhaps, have decided at this point that I am less dedicated to the use of genuine Tonkin cane rods and English reels, gut leaders and historically accurate dry flies, than I am concerned with gobs of worms for catching tidewater eels, lowly hornpout and lethargic suckers. Anything for the makings of a fish chowder.

This is not so.

Above all else, I prefer fly-fishing. My reasons may seem bluntly selfish and less devout than those proclaimed by my purist compatriots; for I enjoy fly-fishing because (1) I can catch more kinds of gamefishes with less muscular effort than by using other tackle or bait; (2) I am always assured of staying within the strictest fishing laws; and (3) since I have done far more fly-casting than any form of angling, I can usually match my peers in executing reasonably long casts, fairly accurately placed.

If I am ever going to show off when fishing, then, it is when I am armed with a true Tonkin cane rod, Hardy reel, double-taper (or forward-taper) fly line and a nine to twelve-foot leader, which I have tied myself and tapered down in the dimensions indicated for a specific kind of fishing. These leaders are not old-style gut. I certainly make concession to the newer synthetic materials that are so manageable. And I believe the finest lines in the world are produced right here in this country.

My choice of bamboo rods depends on weather as much as on the size and species of gamefish I seek. If the wind is blowing I prefer a longer rod, especially on lakes. A medium-length rod is my choice for casting when wading small streams. On windless days and for evening casts when it is still and calm, the rod can hardly be too light to please me—two ounces and less, with matching reel, line, leader and small dry flies.

Of course, at least a medium-length rod and preferably one of eight feet or more is my selection when I cast a sinking line and wet or streamer flies. (This, too, when using poppers for black bass.)

None of the foregoing excludes spin- or baitrod-casting, trolling, or even the use of baits, where these methods are indicated and where they are legally approved.

In a free country, preference rather than dogma should dictate. And angling is, after all, a sport and not a competitive profession for the most of us, thank the Lord. So much for any aspersions about my fishing inclinations.

But I also accept the accusation that I am an excrementitious writer and that one can hardly be denied, on the basis of what I have included in this book so far. A persnickety person would do well to take warning that "you ain't heard nothing yet."

Consider, for instance, a couple of anecdotes from my adolescence. I was working on a daily newspaper at the time this incident took place:

A pulp-paper salesman annually left in the front office a Christmas gift-wrapped box of fine Havana cigars for the male employees and a similarly choice box of chocolates for the girls on our staff. However, we did not get the contents to pass around, for our office manager grabbed off these community-property presents for himself.

He was the kind of individual who would skin a poop for a cent and spoil a knife worth a quarter, as an old saying went. The day before Christmas each year, he told us proudly, he drew a check on his bank for his wife and she wrote one of exactly the same amount for his annual gift. By prearrangement, each thanked the other spouse and promptly at bank opening the day after the holiday, each deposited the money again.

"When anybody asks me what I gave my wife for Christmas, I can boast that I gave her $500, and she can do the same boasting with her friends," he explained.

Well, we decided to do something about the cigars, at least. So one of the boys got together with the mail clerk and when the cigars arrived we borrowed them for a few minutes.

We removed the Havanas and passed them around fairly. Next, we filled the wooden cigar box with dried horse manure, rewrapped it carefully, took it back to the mailing room and later found that, yes, indeed, the manager came in and claimed the "cigars" and toted them home as usual.

One of the men employees boarded with the manager and his wife. An old bachelor, he had paid them well for many years. He described precisely what occurred at the manager's home on Christmas Day.

It seemed that the frugal couple's only daughter had (finally) married a gentleman with whom she worked at a West Coast establishment. She brought her groom home for the holiday season so he could meet her Dad and Mom.

"Geez," the boarding bachelor told us, "it was frightful. Frugality could not be denied! The father-in-law stood up during coffee and mince pie and welcomed the boy into the bosom of his family and presented him with that box of cigars. In the original wrapping, of course!

"Then, so he'd get his own share to smoke, he urged his new son-in-law to 'Open her up right now!'

"You fellows hadn't driven those nails back too tight," the bachelor said, "or, they'd worked loose or something. Anyhow, when that boy pulled off the paper, the cover opened wide and the contents landed smack on the table! Dusted the mince pie, sprinkled the coffee, even fell on the daughter's new hairdo. Everything got a dose!"

We gasped. Somebody asked:

"What was the new son-in-law's reaction?"

The old man told us, "At first his face was as red as his wife's and her parents.' Then he started to laugh and I thought he was going to have hysterics. He got his breath and made what I thought was a classic remark:

" 'Folks,' he said, 'We're going to get along just fine. I've often told my fishing friends that life is too short for anybody to be a horse's ass. Not worth it. Thanks for the gift. It's appropriate."

We grinned in a sickly way, thinking we'd better take that new husband fishing, if we could separate him from his bride; for, once he learned the true nature of his tightwad in-laws, his impression of New Englanders would change drastically.

"He might have got a slant on how it was going to be," our bachelor associate concluded. "The old man blew the dusty droppings off his pie and ate it, regardless."

"Waste not, want not," I thought, laughing.

When I was young and living on a Maine seacoast farm, anybody who went fishing and hunting was considered worthless, just plain no good and destined for a life of wastefulness, sick humor and burial under a smaller stone than his ambitious and hence affluent neighbors. It was all right to fish commercially and to hunt briefly for the family larder but not to enjoy oneself in the business, even then. So we used to sneak off to our favorite streams and lakes, never approach them openly and with declared intent. We met in back of a barn for a convivial drink of hard cider or beer, for even a glass or bottle of spirits was frowned on and social drinking in one's home was unheard-of in those "good old days."

This did give flavor to our clandestine elbow-bending and many an indecorous incident resulted from our casual conversations and our desire to upset the holier concepts of our peers. In speaking of an upright, prosperous fellow-townsman, we summed up his rectitude this way: "He goes to church on Sunday so they call him an honest man."

One never knows what deviltry may result from secret meetings. It has been recorded by at least a few historians that Colonial patriots were less concerned about striking a blow for freedom, when they sneaked into Fort Ticonderoga in the night, than they were about capturing the good liquors stored there by the British. Preplanning showed this as one of the benefits, anyhow, for those woodsmen who had to hike many miles to reach the battle site.

Well, the most successful man in our small neighborhood was a contractor. He not only drove his men hard from daylight to dark but rolled up his own sleeves and pitched right in to set a good example. It went without saying that he didn't waste valuable time fishing for fun. We envied him and at the same time wanted somehow to bring him down a peg publicly. At one back-of-the-barn session, a handy man in our worthless group brought up an interesting subject.

"The first thing done at a new construction site is the placing of an outhouse in a suitable location. Right?"

We agreed.

"So, our esteemed friend always jacks up the privy when a job is done and wheels it to the new building spot. He never builds a new one. No, he carts the old one to wherever he's beginning fresh construction."

We wondered what he was getting at.

He reminded us that the contractor was as regular in his habits as he was thrifty in his business. The old man was the first person in the outhouse mornings and he never missed a

movement, come sun, rain, wind or national disaster. We began to get the crux of the cussedness our friend had conceived when he reminded us:

"The crew just moved everything, including that outhouse,
to the top of the hill right above the center of town. They're
going to build a mansion up there for the contractor. The
road is in already and it drops down, straight as an arrow and
steep as a mountainside, right into town. They haven't had
time to take that backhouse off the wheels. They just got it to
the site by dark this evening. I saw it."

We began to grin.

"I've been hired to do some odd jobs there, starting bright
and early in the morning. I been thinking I should knock the
trigs out from under those wheels about the time the big boss
gets himself well seated. That would let the outhouse roll
down that steep road and fetch up smack in the middle of
things.

"You fellows ought to be in town about then. Somebody is going to need a lot of help righting that two-holer—to say nothing about consolation for our dignified neighbor."

Nobody was needed to clear the road of traffic next day. The screaming and cursing (shocking to righteous men's ears) that came from inside that rolling privy as it gained momentum might have been heard ten miles away.

How people in small towns got away with such deviltry years ago is unimaginable to those who now pay a fine if they fail to see a red light on a crossroad.

Anyway, that small building was well ventilated—if not sanctified—by its swift downhill ride. Its occupant was jarred out of his complacency, too. He even decided to take up occasional fishing, since he'd lost appreciable face as a dignified man with his neighbors.

And the crew gained a new outhouse, for the ancient two-holer was demolished when it turned upside down in the main street, directly opposite the general store.

This left the contractor with his pants down until he got back his equilibrium. He was man enough to join in the

laughter, and what he lost in dignity he gained in conviviality.

It was reminiscent of the story about a righteous, dignified, straight-backed maiden lady who, on her way to church one bright Sunday morning with a friend, took a shortcut across a cow pasture and was heard to exclaim, "Gracious me!"

Her companion asked, "What's the matter?"

Scraping her white-kid shoes on the grass, she became increasingly angry, as was evidenced by this terse response: "Oh! I stepped in some cow-nasty and got my shoe all covered with s--t!"

What has all of the foregoing to do with the question of preferences, or with angling in general? Well, maybe not a hell of a lot, now that you ask. But fish have their preferences, too, and nothing in the early spring will induce more hungry hits from brook trout than the fat white grubs that often lie under drying cow-flaps. Come to think of it, if the lady with the white-kid shoes had preferred to skip church and go fishing, she might have been happier about what turned up for her on that shortcut.

Sometimes, as a bait-fishing boy, I got into a flap myself, but I preferred to turn them over with a shovel, not a shoe, when searching for trout bait.

21

FIFTEENTH QUALIFICATION:

Fortuity

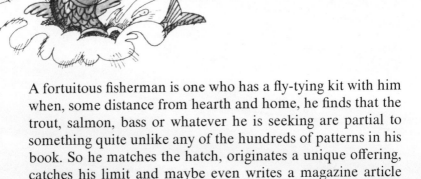

A fortuitous fisherman is one who has a fly-tying kit with him when, some distance from hearth and home, he finds that the trout, salmon, bass or whatever he is seeking are partial to something quite unlike any of the hundreds of patterns in his book. So he matches the hatch, originates a unique offering, catches his limit and maybe even writes a magazine article on the occasion.

A fortuitous fisherman, too, may be an angler who is faced with the need for a solution to a leaky boat or a meal cooked up from next to nothing—but unlike the TV naturalist who puts overripe, winter-killed cranberries on his cereal, or suggests that pine trees are nutritious if not too palatable—a meal I have in mind is something else again, conceived and executed fortuitously at lakeside. A fortuitous fisherman does what he does accidentally on purpose, as it were, if fortune fancies him or frowns. I will put it bluntly: A fortuitous fisherman knows enough to come in out of the rain.

First, that leaky boat.

There were three of us and we had come a long way over a rutted gravel byway in a four-wheel-drive vehicle to reach a mountaintop trout pond. We had been told that a serviceable rowboat was hidden away on the shore and sure enough we soon found this dilapidated craft, rotting away and moss-grown, where its owner had said it would be located. We wondered if we should chance our lives in it but it was a warm day, the water was no colder than it ever is in a spring-fed, glacier-made natural impoundment, and we were all good swimmers.

So, we rigged our rods and tied on dry flies and—one in the bow, one in the stern and the odd man on the center bottom planking, with a bailing can in hand—we shoved off gingerly and made a few trial casts. Soon, both bow and stern fishermen had fat twelve-inch brook trout yanking, sawing and occasionally surfacing on the business ends of our tackle.

But water came in faster than our volunteer bailer could dip and fling it over the side. We boated our trout—one might say, we restocked them in the deepening pool beneath our feet—and decided in the name of common sense to pole ashore.

I was in the stern, so I did the pushing. As the others jumped out on the bank, I noticed that the leak was from a side plank. There was a long split in the cedar and water could, of course, pour in through this crack.

I fished around in my kit and came up with a can of line dressing. It was the consistency of cold butter. I cut a piece from the rope anchor line and, rubbing this with the line dressing, pushed it into the crack a bit at a time. Then I coated the seam thoroughly with the remaining dressing and said:

"Let's, just for the hell of it, give this another try and see if we've accomplished anything."

Our combined weight pushed the crack below the surface, I noted, but no water came in and after we had sopped the moisture from the bottom she didn't leak a drop. The sun dried her out, just dandy. Now, all three of us, by sitting side-wise and casting in unison, were able to fish to our hearts' content. There wasn't any wind, fortunately, and we soon had plenty of trout for a fish-fry ashore, come noon.

Ever since that day, my fishing kit has contained a flat can or two of paste-like line dressing and some strands of oakum or jute. It has surprised me how often these items have come in handy, especially on trips to remote sections of the state.

Canoe-fishing-camping guides always have amberoid or other resin and cloth strips at hand to patch canvas-covered canoes, if leaks have resulted during the day on a rocky river. (Fiberglass repair kits are convenient nowadays, too.) How-ever, even when underway, without taking a canoe or boat from the water, I have plastered greasy line dressing on seams and cracks and stopped leaks quickly and easily.

The fortuitous meal that another fisherman and I had is a second example of how an angler indicates his parents didn't raise any foolish children.

My companion on this foray was drooling over the savory breezes wafting our way from a guide's noon cookout at a picnic site on the shore of the Narrows—a stream-like section of West Grand Lake in Maine.

We had not intended to remain on the lake during lunch and hence had failed to bring anything except a thermos of coffee along in our big Grand Lake canoe. It was one of those rare days, however, when the landlocked salmon and lake trout hit just about every offering. We had returned sev-eral husky fish to the lake but we did have a togue of five or six pounds on a stringer, thinking to give it to our camp cook for a chowder when we returned.

The fishing was so great that not only did landlocks take our trolled streamer flies but, once, I saw a big salmon chas-ing smelts not more than half a cast from our canoe. The fish was close to the surface. It would smash into the smelt school, then arc its broad back and submerge, only to come back up again for more smelts.

I had a second rod all rigged, besides the one I was using

for trolling. So, slowing the motor, I grabbed the extra rod, whipped it briefly and dropped a Gray Ghost streamer in among the thrashing smelts. Then, as it went an inch under, I yanked the fly by lifting my rod tip quickly and WHAM-BANG! I was tied into a beautiful, leaping, running, diving, shaking silversides that put a quivering bow into my bamboo and tested not only any skill I might display but the back-bone of that Tonkin cane, the breaking point of my leader and how firmly the barb was imbedded in the landlock's jaw.

I wanted that salmon. It was one of the heavier landlocks I had fought for a long time. Luck held and before too long I strung the fish beside the laker on our stringer.

The guide and his lunching clients ashore had cheered me on during the contest. With the salmon ours, they picked up their tackle and the guide his cooking utensils. As he came down to the lake for water to extinguish his fire, I told him:

"If we can cook a togue on your fire, we'll make sure to put it out completely."

He told us, "Okay." But his eyebrows lifted when he no-ticed all I carried to the picnic site was the still wiggling la-ker. I grinned.

"Haven't got a little salt and a piece of butter left, have you?" I queried.

"Ayah. Plenty of salt and pepper and a quarter-pound creamery butter." As I reached for my pocketbook, he con-tinued, "No need for that. Camp operator gave me plenty and it'll only melt going back by evening."

So I nonchalantly cut thick fillets from the sides of the togue and, slashing off some green withes, I secured the fil-lets on two slanted pieces of green wood, so they stood in-clined toward the red hardwood coals of his fire, to broil by reflected heat.

When they were thoroughly cooked, I carefully carried them to the picnic table on the large pieces of hardwood. My companion, who had stood staring at the procedure along with the guide and his clients, now spread a couple sheets of paper towel under the sizzling fish.

I opened the butter and divided it equally for our big fillets, sprinkled salt and pepper on the deeply pink fish, and whittled out two thin pieces of pine into the shape of tongue depressors to use for eating utensils.

We either were so hungry that our fillets of lake trout tasted better than Maine lobster, or they actually were all that delicious. Anyway, before we could consume all of the fish, the guide came by and broke away a flake for himself. He tasted it slowly. Then he said:

"Good as any broiled togue I ever have et. You might have used our dishes and silverware. Still, I wanted to see how you were planning to do without them."

"Too lazy to wash dishes," I mumbled, mouthing another chunk of the fish. "Besides, my buddy here was so hungry we couldn't wait to do things the easy way."

He laughed. "Mind if I try another hunk of that togue?"

"You should get something for the use of the fire and for the salt and butter," I replied, smiling.

A fortuitous fisherman, as I suggested earlier, does know enough to come in out of the rain.

There are occasions when the best boat or canoe built is hardly a match for the elements. Then, if an angler is at one end of a lake and his camp or tent is a mile and more at the other end and, if a sudden thunderstorm or vicious summer squall occurs, he's better off getting wet ashore than drowning in a swamped craft.

I well recall, too, the speed with which a Maine bush pilot veered away from a hail storm over the northern wilderness of that state. My first experience took place when the wings of small, pontoon-equipped planes were thin and readily penetrated by such driving hail. We weren't about to get caught in that, he told me, after we had landed on the first piece of water large enough to take the little ship safely.

I have waited out many storms since then, when either boat or plane was my conveyance. The trite truism, "better late than never," certainly applies in such situations in wilderness fishing trips.

So, many of the tragic incidents that anglers experience are not "accidents" at all. It is like the sign over a motel parking area that another fisherman and I encountered once when we were visiting a saltwater beach resort to do some predawn casting for striped bass. The patronage, as well as the management, were French-Canadian and the language therefore might be garbled a bit.

In this instance, some of the kids apparently had tossed baseballs around and maybe broken a few windows. But we happened to read the sign just as an attractive French girl walked under it on her way to sunbathe on the sand below or perhaps to swim in the ocean.

I read the words aloud and precisely as they were painted on the board she walked beneath:

"Do not play with balls. Could cause *accident.*"

"And the bait-dealers at this beach have 'Bait for strip-pers'—not for stripers," my angling companion told me, pointing his finger at another sign.

"I wonder," he went on, "if a nine-foot rod is legal for catching strippers, down this-a-way?"

22

THE QUEST FOR

Perfection– of a Sort

Sympathy, if not outright admiration, for the little individual, the undistinguished person, the humble, everyday kind of angler, has been expressed frequently in this book. It is a trait of the so-called "solid citizens" of New England to express pride for any achievement, to have come up from small beginnings, and to apologize for any acquisition which—morally, socially and, especially financially—puts one above the common man.

For one thing, a newly painted house means an increase in valuation and thus requires additional taxes. So if an old Yankee improves his property, he has the work done inside his home, where it won't be obvious to tax assessors. And he doesn't want his friends and neighbors to think he is trying to excrete above his anus, as an old saying goes (although it's often put more bluntly).

I think my youngest brother expressed this viewpoint succinctly when he was asked by a new acquaintance if he was
related to Bill Elliot, the baritone singer, and Bob Elliot, the
writer.

"Yup. Both are my brothers."

"Well, what do you do to distinguish yourself, John?"

"Oh," he replied, "I'm just a humble carpenter, like Christ
was."

So, even if he is an exceptionally fine cabinetmaker and
craftsman, John realizes that perfection in any field is not
possible for humankind, only for the gods.

In fishing, can we cast repeatedly without ever experienc-
ing a backlash? Can we always play a gamefish to net or gaff
without breaking leader or line? Can we never fail to place
lure or fly precisely over a trout, salmon, bass or perch?

We may learn near-perfection and acquire adequate ability in any activity, including angling. But there's many a slip
between the cup and the lip, as the older generation often
phrased it. This includes fishing, certainly, and it excludes
perfection in writing about angling, as well as concerning
more ordinary life patterns.

Once, I wrote fiction. I followed a formula to achieve yarns
that might interest editors. For example, a fictitious situation
was planned in which a man fell into a well. By his own ingenuity, not by chance, he climbed almost out of the hole.
Then, having reached a climax in the tale, he fell back in and
things appeared very dark, indeed. However, he quickly sur-
mounted this crisis and soon stood outside the well, for the
happy, exciting ending.

I learned of an actual situation which, it seemed to me,
achieved all of these essential elements to make a perfect
story. (It turned out I wrote a bit ahead of my time; for this
was years ago and sex was hardly a subject for national
magazines, except in those pocket-size cartoon booklets like
Captain Billy's Whiz-Bang, which used such daring quickies
as: "Mary has a little lamb, it's fleece is snowy white . . . but
Mary's lamb doesn't stand a chance, when Mary's calf's in
sight." Mary was stepping up into a streetcar and her dress

had climbed almost to her knee in the picture accompanying this ditty.) We hid such jokebooks from the sensitive eyes of our girl friends, believe me, in those moral days.

Anyhow, my tale concerned a young man of marriageable age and inclination who had, indeed, already given a girl an engagement ring. Then his father took him aside and confessed that he was the father of the girl and, hence, the marriage would be incest. "She's your half sister," the errant parent admitted, shamefacedly.

When the youth moped around the house and his mother wanted to know why, he finally told her of the old man's guilt. (Now we are at the climax of the yarn, see?)

And here's the happy ending:

The mother's brow clouded darkly and she said, "Son, you go ahead and marry that girl. That dirty old man ain't your father, anyway!"

Having been brought up by a strict, go-to-church-on-Sunday parent myself, I never could quite comprehend how liberal-living no-goods like the characters described above could be such capable outdoorsmen oftentimes. Yet they were typical of those who fished and made love all summer and, come cold weather, stopped fishing.

So they really approached perfection in dual roles, even if perfection were unattainable.

And there were many of the back-country folks whose hearts were as big as silicone-treated breasts are nowadays. They would give you the shirts off their backs, but you might want to launder such a gift before putting it on, as modern plumbing hadn't then replaced the old sheet-iron washtub for Saturday-night baths.

I was in the mountainous north of New Hampshire years ago, to try my luck at trout fishing in streams adjacent to the Quebec boundary. The trail led past a typical woodsman's log cabin. As I walked along in the light from a rising sun, the man of the house opened his door and urged me to come in and have a bite with his family. The aroma of coffee was too tempting to pass up, so I accepted his neighborly offer.

When I stepped inside, three or four kids dashed across

the cabin floor and scooted up a ladder to a loft above. They were as shy as wild things. Looking up, I could see a row of eyes staring down at me through the sizable cracks in the attic floor.

Their mother was patting out dough for biscuits and I waited in anticipation for her to cook them. I knew they'd be feather-light; they'd be spread with wild strawberry jam and would melt in my mouth.

Just then, I heard hens cackling wildly in the loft above and the cries of excited kids, now over their shyness and back playing games.

Their mother shouted: "You little devils stop running around up there! You're knocking down hen manure into my biscuit dough!"

How could a poor, big-hearted woman hope to achieve perfection under such adverse conditions? Any more than I might experience a perfect day's fishing?

So I wasn't too surprised when brook trout did not strike my wet flies, even though I gave them what was (and still is) a good combination in northern New England: two Dark Montreal wets, Size 12. One on the end of the leader and the other tied in on a dropper a foot or so above the first fly. I first saw this cast presented by a French-Canadian river guide whom I had employed to run me down the Allagash Waterway. (This means going north, since the Allagash River flows in that compass direction.)

We had stopped for a break on a gravel bar. There were two small brooks coming into confluence with the main river at that point. The current was strong, but shallow water flowed over visible sand and stones. I picked up my fly rod and started to cast small dry patterns that had good flotation. When I didn't catch any trout, the guide assembled an ancient glass rod and tied the two Montreals to a level leader as described above. His initial cast—or what looked more like a tossing heave—swung down with the current a short distance before he began to take in line. Now he lifted his rod and, in a swinging arc, tossed a pair of eight-inchers onto the gravel bar.

Soon successive casts and flings put fish aplenty on the sand for our lunch.

Since I hadn't felt a hit, I walked over to examine his rig. Subsequently, I was to become convinced of the efficacy of casting two wet Montreals, rather than a single fly of any pattern or size, when fishing the rivers of northern New England and adjacent Canada. Indeed, to return to an earlier style of fishing, casts of three flies at a time were equally effective, if not more so, in this part of the country.

So, today, I tried to take trout by using not just two Montreals but putting out a three-fly cast in some of the better pools that I had nearly always found productive. Nothing doing. My presentations may have approached perfection—like the biscuits sprinkled with chicken droppings—but if so the trout lacked appreciation of my fishing finesse just then.

It had been a hot, unusually dry spring. Water was low. While the weather was pleasant and sunshiny that day, as it had been for weeks past, rain was sorely needed. A threat of woods closing existed, I knew, to prevent fires. Perfection in weather, then, when it comes to catching trout, doesn't necessarily apply, either.

Toward noon I was ready to retrace my steps and call it a day.

As I munched a sandwich and drank water from a woodland spring, I noticed the sky was darkening. Then thunder rolled and echoed in the heavens. Lightning flashed. A violent rainstorm beat down through the trees and bounced off the river like millions of buckshot bombarding the water. I took refuge under a windfall that sometime before might have been felled by lightning like the flashes now splitting the sky apart. It lay on an angle, with its top on a hillside, so I had room to stand nearly upright under its still-green foliage.

From my shirt pocket I removed a sheet of plastic and draped it over my head, so it fell to the ground like an elongated poncho. (I usually keep such sheeting for these emergencies. It weighs next to nothing, isn't too bulky, and can be handy to have along when afield.) Aside from the threat of being struck by lightning, then, I wasn't too uncomfortable or apprehensive. Indeed, the storm broke as quickly as it had formed.

With the quick change in water temperature, trout became active and it didn't matter what I cast that afternoon: Anything would take fish. Whereas I hadn't experienced a rise earlier in the day, several trout at once now would rise and smash at a fly as soon as it hit the water.

This was as close to perfect fishing as I ever had known. (On occasion, when rainfall has been continuous for several weeks, perhaps, a sudden clearing and bright sunshine will likewise cause trout and other gamefishes to strike.)

I was so pleased with myself that afternoon in northern New Hampshire that I stopped at the log cabin where I'd had coffee and hot hen-manure biscuits earlier and gave the woman a mess of trout for the family supper.

"Take along the rest of these biscuits," she insisted. "I cooked more than we ate this morning. They aren't too bad cold."

As I hiked the rest of the trail back to my car, I thought of the old joke about the fussy female who, in an unfamiliar restaurant, asked the waitress, "What's your special?"

"We've got some good tongue . . ."

"Oh, no! I couldn't eat anything that came out of a cow's mouth. Oh, no! Give me a couple of boiled eggs. Nice fresh ones, right from the hens."

Perfection? The Perfect Piscator? There well may have been "A Compleat Angler" in old Ike Walton's day, I wouldn't know. A fisherman loses faith in the light of current national events. Anyhow, despite many claims that assume perfection piscatorially, I personally have yet to achieve—or to meet anybody else who has achieved—such perfection as to take a trout on every cast, a sucker on every worm, a laker on every spoon, a catfish on every jug-bait. When we reach that kind of paradise, I anticipate perfection will be a pile-like pain in the posterior.

23

Identification

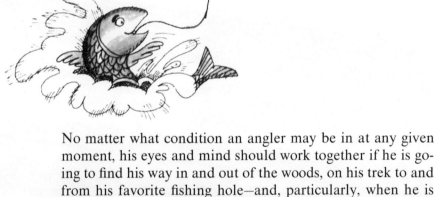

No matter what condition an angler may be in at any given moment, his eyes and mind should work together if he is going to find his way in and out of the woods, on his trek to and from his favorite fishing hole—and, particularly, when he is exploring new fishing waters reached over unfamiliar terrain.

A piscatorial colleague of mine got himself lost in New York City following an hours-long cocktail party, once upon a time. In the predawn darkness he was like the inebriate who repeatedly banged his forehead into a telephone pole and finally exclaimed: "Lost! Lost, by God, in the impenetrable forest!"

My pal used his head to think out the objects his eyes identified and, lacking a compass, to see telephone poles as he would have seen trees in the northwoods. Thus, he asked another late reveler: "Say, Man, what side of these light poles does the moss grow on here in the city?"

Then, knowing this much, he took a northerly course and ultimately reached his destination. (After a police patrol car had him as a passenger for a while, that is.)

In the big woods, nevertheless, there may not be helping hands of the law behind every tree—although to a fisherman who transgresses by catching an over-limit, this well may appear to be the case. Usually, an angler must depend on himself, or a guide. If the guide takes a wrong turn, as some of them well may do, then the essentials in a fisherman's kit help them to find their way out of a dilemma. These items are a good compass and a topographical map. Just any old general map of an area is not good enough. The map must be detailed and accurate.

Lost outdoorsmen find themselves worrying. Often, to add to their concern, a cold, steady rain will fall and drench them to such a degree it might seem that whole multitudes of angels in the heavens above were afflicted with peeing diabetes.

Thus, a careful sportsman, hiking into the unknown, will blaze a trail which he can follow out again. This is more dependable than map and compass but, in case he wanders away from the blazes, he still needs both items.

Now, it may seem unbelievable, yet there are anglers who do not realize that the axe cuts or broken branches must be pointing in the opposite direction from the way they advance into a fishing location. Coming out again, these signs must be seen in reverse of any blazes that show the trail leading to the stream or lake. One walks past a tree and, looking back the way he has come, he bends a branch or cuts a shallow notch at eye level, to show him the way home. (Fishing-lodge operators and guides usually mark trees in both directions by cutting blazes and then even by painting the slashes with bright red or some other color, so anybody can walk back into remote waters and find his way home, even if the trails have grown up with brush after clearing.)

Experienced outdoorsmen often pick a peculiarly shaped

tree, a taller-than-average tree, an exposed boulder or similar object, and store such markers in their memories to be brought up like signposts when needed. Again, if they are hiking into an unfamiliar section, they still must look back and study such markers from the angle they will appear on the way out of the woods, as well as on the way in.

When a fisherman makes canoe or float trips along waterways in wilderness areas, he frequently encounters places where the main branch of a river spreads out into a pondlike, perhaps marshy, impoundment. Drifting along, he sees that a choice of two streams lies at the outlet of the little lake. Maybe there is an island in the middle of the river and the water splits to eddy around both sides of this isle.

It is well to choose the outlet with the faster current, but if both streams appear to be of equal movement and the fisherman starts down the wrong channel, he usually will realize his mistake shortly, as the stream narrows and becomes increasingly shallow. Then he must retrace his way by poling, motoring, or pulling and hauling his craft back up to the confluence of the waterways and trying his luck in the opposite channel. Again, as in the walking woods, the liquid paths of a back-country river are more readily identified from a definitive map and the direction affirmed by use of a good compass.

There are sources where charts are obtainable, of course. In the New England region, The Appalachian Mountain Club, 5 Joy Street, Boston, Mass. 02108, has an excellent pocket-sized hardcover book, the *A.M.C. New England Canoeing Guide,* for a modest charge. This is valuable especially when canoeing and fishing wilderness rivers.

It is not only the eyes and mind, but the *ears,* too, which warn an angler of dangerous rapids ahead. I am reminded of the debutante who had spent all of her summers with her wealthy parents at their home on the Maine seacost. She was intrigued by all males but particularly by men in uniform. So, when a seasonal police officer, whom she had not yet conquered, was home from college and directing traffic in a resort town's main street, the deb stopped her sports car beside him and coyly asked:

"Officer, where is Smith's Garage?"

He told her, smiling: "Oh, have they moved it, Gail? Last time I looked it was in the same location where we've always found it."

She said: "Oh, you!" And thus began a ripening romance—rapids or no rapids ahead.

Yes, I have found that identification of objects material to outdoor experiences is consequential, to say the least.

Speaking of which, there was an aging angler who went to his dentist to have an ulcerous tooth removed. He shook his head at the novocaine.

"I've had such bad pain recently that a tooth hauling is nothing," he told the doctor. "Just haul her out."

The dentist remonstrated, knowing the hurt he would have to cause, but the old man insisted and the doctor yanked and twisted until the molar came free.

The ancient angler never quivered.

"What kind of pain, for heaven's sake, has been so bad you don't mind an extraction like this?" the dentist wanted to know.

"Wal," the old man said, "I was fishing up north and stopped to stoop behind a tree for my morning movement, when I sat down on the open jaws of a bear trap and sprung it—bang-snap."

"Lord! That must have hurt!"

"Yeah," the patient agreed, "but, you know how they fasten the trap by a chain and drive the end of the chain into a big log? Wal, if you think the jaws of that trap snapping shut was painful, you should have heard me holler when I came to the end of the chain!"

In addition to being able to identify land and water terrain, bear traps and garages, too, it is helpful in the making of an angler to get to know at a glance the difference between a brook trout and a blacknose shiner; a bullhead and a perch; a togue and a tuna. And, fishing elsewhere than in waters that support the foregoing species, to learn both local and scientific nomenclature for gamefishes being sought. This adds prestige to a fisherman's standing among his peers.

It keeps back enthusiastic declarations like *"C'est Magnifique!"* if somebody serves *Catostomus commersoni* (white sucker) instead of salmon, with you as a guest. A mild response to the host's "How do you like it?" should be used instead. Something in the nature of "Hmmm" will do.

Once, living on a Maine farm as a boy, I visited neighboring youths whose father had spilled kerosene oil on the flour while driving his horse home from the country store. Things were tough all around and the mother and wife was not about to throw out the flour, regardless. It seems to me that I can still taste the bread, cake, pies and cookies we ate that long-ago weekend.

Yes, identification of fishing pals can be equally important as making trail signs to trout streams. Sucker soup and petroleum patties identify those with whom I fish nevermore. Never, nevermore.

24

SEVENTEENTH QUALIFICATION:

Discrimination

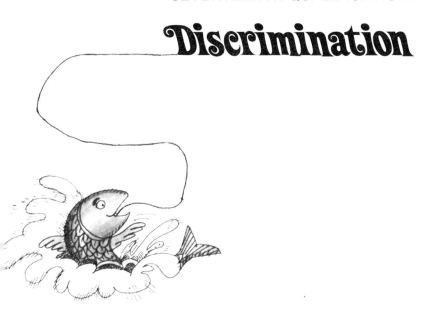

Somebody once remarked that it is a good thing everyone's fancy for the opposite sex does not include identical criteria; otherwise all girls would want the same man and all men would pursue a single female. We are fortunate our peculiar fantasies cause us to discriminate to a degree that allows pairings-off to nearly everybody's marital satisfaction—for a while, at least.

So it is with fishing. One angler may prefer to spin-cast for bass, another to fly-fish for salmon, while a third sportsman sees pike as his preference. Freshwater species may hold allure for large numbers of piscators; a similar number think small fishes are for the birds and that the supreme sport is in hooking and playing giant ocean gamefishes like tuna, swordfish and sharks.

So be it.

Doubtless our individual background plays a role in our choice of species and the kind of tackle we prefer to fish with. In the making of an angler, my own fondness for trouting with a dry fly has resulted, I am certain, from reading books and magazine articles on the subject for many years—glowing words that give the trout taken on some historic and authentic bit of fluff a certain prestige rarely accorded to any other species, except it be a sea-run salmon. Also, from having lived most of my life thus far in states that have had populations of truly wild, not stocked, trout. (*Salvelinus fontinalis,* the Eastern brook trout, that is; brown trout and rainbows have been largely planted species.)

The trout, I have found, is pursued by a rather prestigious piscatorial person, an individual who thinks that Tonkin cane rods are not only preferable to those built from more modern materials, but that cane rods are a requirement (as are dry flies of early origin) to distinguish him as a qualified member of an exclusive fraternity. He is rarely seen without this kind of equipment. Along with a Norfolk jacket, waders with cleated soles and, above all, an ancient fishing hat that is thoroughly adorned with flies stuck into a band of lamb's wool. Most of the true dry-fly trouters smoke a pipe and the truly ethical members of the clan prefer a curved stem on their briars.

Now, one may encounter just any old fisherman, out in pursuit of other kinds of gamefishes, with a chaw of tobacco in his swollen cheek and a pint of rum in his hip pocket. Not so, the genuine trouter. He drinks his spirits in the evening, from glasses decorated with paintings by recognized wildlife artists. For, unlike the everyday fisherman, the trouter returns to his log-cabin clubhouse at night, oftentimes, while the run-of-the-mill angler is prone to day trips that get him back to home and business after the sun has set.

There are times, of course, when sportsmen make extended treks into wildernesses in search of pike, muskies and lakers. However, the trout-seeker is "away" with his kind even if his retreat be but twenty miles from his permanent abode.

Times change grudgingly for those who pursue the brook trout. Nowadays, not everybody effects an English accent simply because his tackle dates back to the turn of the century. (The come-latelies may not even be Ivy Leaguers and they have been known to appear on location with rods and reels produced right here in this country. Yet this is rarely so and they are accorded pitying glances and it may be said among old-timers: "Looks like just anybody is acceptable now.")

A brook-trouter who fishes dry may keep a breakfast trout or two but limit catches are frowned on and highly ethical anglers return all fish to the water.

In one club, I was informed that it was unsportsmanlike to allow the current to give a dry fly motion—let alone to jiggle one's rod and thus bounce the pattern about a bit on the surface. Casting was supposed to be done across pools and, when the fly began to move, it must be immediately picked up and recast. If a fish struck when the fly hit the water, well and good. Otherwise, no tricks, please.

With the advent of sinking lines for casting bushy streamers and more delicate nymphs, purists have gradually given way to their less aesthetic fellows and the wild Eastern brook trout, too, has declined in population if not in popularity. Other kinds of trout are found over a much wider area of this country—for waters in many sections are too warm now to support the speckled char that was mistaken by English colonists for the brown trout they had known in their island streams.

Yet some of us diehards cling to our idealism, which is nearer idolatry for this fascinating fish. It is as though we had ichorous ethereal fluid flowing in our veins, as it was supposed to have run in the arteries of mythological Greek gods. I have sometimes fought against this inherent snobbery by returning to bait and cane pole, but never when fishing for that noble aquatic resident of cool springs and shaded pools, the wild, mysterious Eastern brook trout.

Again, I have laughed at myself and poked fun at other idolaters but in the recesses of my mind I inevitably romanticize *Salvelinus fontinalis* and occasionally turn to verse to express the emotional warmth I feel for the speckled trout.

With words like these:

TO TAKE A TROUT*

(There is no wind this evening;
Reflected in the quiet pool
The trees are upside-down.)

This is a time for fishing
With feathers light as down;
To use a floating fly line,
And a leader finely drawn;
A rod that's built of Tonkin cane,
As weightless as a wand.

(The mayflies now are hatching,
And the trout are going wild.)

This is the time to place a fly
Precisely where that big one rose;
To let it lie: then move it . . .Ah!
He comes up from the bottom
And tears apart the sky
Reflected in the quiet pool!
This is a time for fishing
Exquisitely dry.
                              —*Bob Elliot*

Many sportsmen, who have fished only occasionally, and then largely for stocked brook trout instead of the wild fish of our northern wilderness waters, declare that this species is the easiest of all trouts to catch and creel. Personally, I have not found it such a willing prey. Nor have I noticed that my fishing friends are capable of getting strikes on every cast in those places where diminishing populations of wild brook

*From "There's No Fishing Like Flyrod Fishing," Copyright 1972 by the Cortland Line Company. (Published by Richards Rosen Press, Inc., 29 E. 21st St., NYC 10010.)

trout dwell. Nevertheless, I agree that those of us who are devoted to speckled brookies above all other gamefishes, need to be "brought down a peg" now and again.

When a fellow member of an exclusive club told me he had met a "wonderful sportsman" the winter before, while vacationing in the South, and that the man had said I knew him personally, since he came from my home town, I asked his name.

"He's a highly successful businessman. Has some kind of a city contract, I believe. Name is H. R. Jones. He impressed me as a really prestigious fellow; just the kind of person we need in our trouting fraternity."

I smiled. "Yes, he's a capable fisherman and a good neighbor. That contract? It's for collecting the city garbage. Pays well. He can afford the club membership fee. Might need to check now and then to make certain his flies are the artificial kind. Lots of the live ones follow him around on collection days."

I thought, as he wrinkled his thin patrician nose, "Who the hell do we think we are, anyhow? Do we actually believe we are better individuals simply because we cast flies instead of plugs; use feathers and fur instead of worms? Can it be that our snobbery shows on the outside?"

In our fireside conversations, we wonder if the end is near for the kind of exclusive angling we have enjoyed—not just because trout and salmon are less abundant than they once were, but also because the public is intruding on our aristocratically peaceful pastures and ponds. If we purists really consider that we are superior beings, it well may be time to reevaluate our lofty perches.

Once I stopped on the shore of a mountainside pond to chat with an elderly man while he framed the roof of a new log cabin. I wondered at first if he was like some old-timers who, when a shelter began to fall apart and the litter and garbage was piled high, decided it was easier to erect a new camp than to put up with the old one any longer. However, he told me this story:

"My wife and I got along fine until our daughter entered

high school in the village down in the valley. Then the two of them joined forces against me. First thing, I had to add screens to keep out the black flies—even though the insects are only vicious in the spring, as you know.

"Next, I had to send to Rosy-Searsbuck for a chemical toilet, although the old outhouse warn't but a few years old. That was a comfortable two-holer, too. Hated to give her up. I'd even fitted the openings to suit our behinds individually, by drawing pencil marks around my wife's rear-end as she squatted on the seat-board and having her draw around mine. Softest wood I could find was used in the seat. Smoothed it down with wood rasp and sandpaper 'til it was like sitting on velvet.

"Guess what really licked me was the time I went out there in the evening, as usual, but had a bit of bad luck. It was a full, bright, moonlight night, see, and I didn't take a lantern with me, as I normally would have done. Come time to clean up and I had to fish around for paper, I recall. Got back into the cabin and stood there scrubbing my hands with yellow soap and water and my wife said:

" 'You've been going out there every night since we were married. Never saw you wash your hands afterwards until tonight. Don't understand it.'

" 'You'd wash yours,' I told her, 'if you'd wiped your ass on a moonbeam!'

"She used that as an opening wedge to get the inside chemical closet. One thing adds to another, when you give in to women." He spattered tobacco juice on a cedar log. Then he told me:

"Girl's graduating from high school next month. Some of her friends will be up the mountain to visit her, like as not, she and my wife figure. So they have to have this new log cabin to show off in. Sure beats hell, don't it?"

25

EIGHTEENTH QUALIFICATION:

Lest some Ms. resent my earlier chapter about the Honey-moon Bucktail Fly, I emphasize herewith that any slighting reference to fisherwomen should be taken lightly. I am not a misogynist, by any means. Indeed, I appreciate the viewpoint of one old-timer who agrees that a sleeping bag is okay but that he much prefers one who stays awake on any camping-fishing expedition.

The word "tolerance" in this chapter's heading really shouldn't be applied to the modern Ms. who may chance to enjoy piscatorial pastimes. If there's anything a today's gal is angry about, it is being simply tolerated by man. My excuse is this: I grew up in an era when marriages were made in heaven and berths (sic) were made in sleeping cars. I don't blame the feminine gender for seeking liberation. But on the fishing front, do they have to do the whole job so much better than mere men that we get egg on our faces instead of trout scales?

Once I covered a sportsmen's show in Boston and the promoters conceived the idea of a nationally famous fly caster (male) teaching an internationally known golfer (female) how to throw a tapered line the length of a big indoor pool.

This caster could write his name in the air with a fly line. He had fished with a President. He had matched skills in actual fishing and exhibition casting with every known challenger and always had come out on top. His touch was delicately artistic. The line seemed to float away from the rod tip without any effort except a gentle movement of his wrist. Now he was a gray-haired, distinguished individual, recognized as an artist for his oil paintings and sought out for his realistic fish mountings.

The golfer watched him weave the rod lightly and toss the line to the pool's end. Then, as he handed her the bamboo "stick" and offered to place his fingers on her wrist, to transfer his rhythm to her hand, she stepped aside and said into a microphone for the crowd:

"An idiot could cast this thing. An athlete doesn't need instruction in such a simple sport. I've never done it in my life but—" (Here she grabbed the fly rod from his hands) "—watch this!"

She matched his act to perfection. Not only did the line reach the end of the pool but her first cast placed its end far beyond, up on a platform 20 feet farther than the professional artist had dropped his line.

Then she turned and walked disdainfully away. The fly caster looked like a chastised boy. Somebody whose mother had mopped the floor with him.

There are men who would enjoy ruining somebody else's act in a similar way, of course. This gal definitely was the exception but she had competed against others for so long that any exhibition meant winning, for her.

Competition is creeping into sport fishing. Yet a great majority of both men and women anglers still continue to fish for fun, not profit or trophies. Modesty, humility and even self-abasement are qualities of the quiet people who enjoy participant activities on stream and lake everywhere. Happiness can be letting a man teach his gal how to put a worm on a hook and when she knows how to do it just as well herself, to ask him to keep on doing this for her.

Most men, particularly those inclined toward outdoor sports, put women on a pedestal; they don't want a pal but a pleasant, pretty, helpless fishing partner. When the man has shown her how, then she may evince capabilities to prove to him that he's an excellent instructor.

Ms., this isn't a book about aggressions. I, we, he, they love you. Try us and see how responsive we can be. I am reminded of the game warden who saw a pretty girl fishing in a brook for trout. The limit lengthwise was six inches—not too large a brookie—but the law was rigorously enforced unless there were extenuating circumstances. Like a beautiful fisherwoman?

Well, when she saw the warden approaching, she took three or four short-length trout from her straw creel and slid them down inside her rubber boots.

The warden saw what she had done but, instead of accusing her and hauling her into court, he stood and chatted with her for half an hour. The sun glinted off the water and beat down on her booted legs, ripening the hidden trout. Her flesh crawled with the sticky slime. She was about ready to tell him she preferred to pay a fine and lose her license when he finally relented and walked away, smiling.

She never broke a fishing law again.

One old guide told me that several years ago he was out with a sportsman who was obviously enamored of a girl who could fish, cook outdoors, shoot, paddle a canoe, run an outboard motor and, indeed, do anything a man could do.

"Just as well or better."

The sportsman was married, the guide knew, but he talked so much about this perfect outdoorswoman that the guide wondered how long the marriage might last. He saw his chance to show the sportsman that his ideal girl was human, after all, and to knock her off the pedestal she occupied in the sportsman's mind.

"She even rides horseback beautifully," the sportsman rhapsodized.

"Now," the old guide advised, with unsmiling face and fatherly concern, "that's one thing I wouldn't want in a female. When it comes to horseback, that's stretching things too far, the way I see it."

The sportsman swore softly. His romance was ruined, then and there, the guide well knew. But just to be certain the grizzled guide went on:

"Women really are wonderful. None of us would be here without them. The world would be one hell of a mess if mothers didn't show their sons how to grow up with at least a bit of morality and common sense. Think what it would be like if there were only men to foul up the earth. But there's one thing three men can do that two women can't do properly. That's urinate in a single toilet at the same time. Men sure have a handy little thing to take on a picnic, as the saying goes, huh?"

So, it is tolerance for men who go fishing when they might be gainfully employed—tolerance on the part of women for errant males—that I prefer as a subject of this chapter. A bit of understanding by both sexes is my general idea.

When it comes to tying tiny flies, the small, delicate hands of our gals often are more adaptable to the job than our own hairy paws. In fishing lodges, too, feminine niceties can transform rum-drinking, tobacco-chewing sessions into pleasant, fastidious cocktail hours and there's nothing wrong with change of this kind, it seems to me.

"I once knew a man who took engaged couples aside and, in a fatherly voice, advised them how to achieve a happy state of marriage," an old guide recalled as we fished for bass on a warm June day.

"Both partners have to learn to give and take," was how the guide summed up the self-appointed counselor's marital advice.

"Only thing was," the guide continued with a grin, "the old cuss was married to a real shrew who never let him call his soul his own. So he had to both give *and* take it, himself."

He pointed silently at a patch of pickerel weeds and I cast a black bass plug right where he meant for me to drop it. A largemouth came up and struck hard. As I applied pressure, the fish leaped and splashed, dove, sounded and then came off the bottom with a drive that broke the surface and lifted him skyward like the takeoff of a rocket from its launching pad. Then, glistening body curved, water dropping from its dark scales like rain, the bass plunged into the lake again and ran off yards of line before I could take up the slack. The fish and I made contact simultaneously—both his lunging motion and my sudden thumbing of the reel spool creating tension that could have but one result: a broken leader.

He came up once more; then in a final splash that was accompanied by a savage, angry head-shaking, he freed himself from the plug, tossing it on the surface, as if to inform me: "Take this imitation back and don't ever try to fool me again with anything like it."

We scooped it up. I stammered an expression that must have been stored in my subconsciousness since I was a high school kid on the New Hampshire seacoast, where language took strange forms, at times.

"Jeest, Bub!" I exclaimed, "Warn't that a godda!"

26

NINETEENTH QUALIFICATION:

Enthusiasm

There is compatibility between fishermen that allows agreement in exaggeration and that understands enthusiasm for the catching of a six-inch trout or perch.

Once a friend of mine would tell people, "I caught a pike that long!"—extending his arms as wide as they would reach. Then, turning his back on his listeners, and drawing his hands together so perhaps a foot showed between them, he would substantiate his tale by saying: "Didn't I, Joe?"

And, Joe would nod solemnly in affirmation.

Well, after a period of years, an angler not only begins to believe his own wild yarns about the size and number of gamefishes he has hooked and played, but he also imparts such enthusiasm to audiences large and small, that they, too, credit his lies. To a point of wanting to go to the waters the angler has fished and trying to imitate his successes, real or imaginary. Family budgets suffer depletion to pay for trips to far-away destinations and nobody admits on returning that there has been anything but similarly incredible action for trout, bass, salmon, pike, muskies, sailfish, tarpon or tuna, or whatever the quarry might be.

Nobody believes a politician but everybody's eyes bulge, everybody's pulse quickens, everybody's mind boggles and everybody's reaction is envious, when fishermen recount their latest adventures.

There came a time, of course, when non-anglers expressed wonderment that we failed to bring home the fillets if not the bacon. So, ethics entered to solve this dilemma.

"I put 'em all back in the water. Caught fifty trout and returned them to grow another day.

"I believe in saving fish for my sons and grandsons. If everybody keeps all he catches, there won't be any left for little Jack and Henry."

This has been a marvelous receptacle, a vessel in which the three small fishes of Biblical times might well have brought forth fillets for five thousand hungry persons. The narration, anyhow, is hardly less credible than those accounts of modern-day anglers whose exploits do not even bear a heavenly blessing.

But who is hurt by the enthusiastic exaggerations of pleasantly smiling piscatorial companions? The joy of angling, indeed, well may be enhanced by such fishing fantasies. Surely tackle companies, outdoor writers, fishing guides, boat-builders, manufacturers of motors, depth finders, paddles and oarlocks, to say nothing of magazine and book publishers, all profit rather than lose from the exaggerator's tall tales.

Can anybody imagine clubs or state and federal agencies being able to rear and stock heavily enough to assure a fish in everyman's frypan?

So, again, a latterly attitude among us is one which sees attributes in angling besides fish: the fresh air, blue skies, singing birds, wildlife—even dusty dirt roads that lead through evergreen trees to quiet places which should and perhaps may hold a trout or two; who knows? Now, a rare but occasional individual may even tell the truth and admit: "Didn't catch any fish but had a wonderful time."

The joy of casting is of itself a rewarding pastime with all of the fine tackle available nowadays. How often an old guide has had to remind a client:

"Can't catch any fish in the air. Weaving that line and lure overhead may be fun and prove you can heave them a long way; but the fish are still in the water. No flying fish hereabouts, friend."

The response is: "Fish are not all that important to me. I just enjoy being out and listening to your lies about the good old days."

Thus, an angler in the making may well be a person who becomes reconciled to persisting despite his pessimism and, when good luck strikes, then he is exultant.

Once, I caught a single creditable fish in two days of determined angling. I showed off the trophy and described the action until a friend in camp exclaimed: "He lands one keeper in 48 hours of fishing and talks our ears off! If he caught a legal limit, he'd go on national television."

Nevertheless, there are occasions when fish strike at nearly every cast; when they hit trolled baits and lures consistently; when the action is so fast that an angler becomes arm-weary, even bored by it all.

During annual trips to New Bedford, Massachusetts, with a couple of friends, I have hauled aboard sriped bass and bluefish until the sport was simply hard work. I recall a captain who sold his catch ashore; his fee was reduced if we caught a given poundage, and we seldom failed to locate feeding saltwater species before the day was done. Fighting fish of from six to perhaps 30 pounds; pumping the rod, then reeling line; pumping again and reeling in a bit more; the strong fish hanging in a running tide and the boat underway—if slowly—we knew we were involved in something that made arms, back and soft muscles from head to toe ache to near-exhaustion.

I have occasionally hit schools of pollock, mackerel and

similar ocean species and have hardly been able to keep up with the action, too. Handlining from head boats off the New England seacoast, I have brought up from the bottom husky cod, haddock, hake, cusk and outsize pollock in apparently endless numbers. Then, with others aboard, I've gone without a strike for hours at a time. The boredom of too many fish is about as tiresome as none at all, it seems to me.

Except for those warm-water species in the South and, more rarely, New England bass, pickerel, perch and smelts, the inland fishing we know today can be slow more often than fast. When trout, salmon and lakers are the quarry, a lot of luck and at least a minimum of skill are necessary if we are to back up the yarns we have spread abroad about the wonderful fishing in our bailiwick. Oh, the satisfaction of having full cooperation from fish, when we take a friend to that secret location, about which we have bragged so often in his hearing!

I remember once when I had enticed a magazine editor and his publisher to come to Maine and dry-fly-fish for brook trout in a northerly wilderness pond. Everything went so well on that trip that they never stopped talking about it and always wanted to return for a similar fishing session with me. But, knowing how fortunate we had been, I was reluctant to take another chance. Only once more did the editor come back and our luck was divided on his second expedition, as I will describe here later. The publisher is still holding a rain-check on a repeat visit.

That first time, I met the two men in western Maine and drove them to Greenville on the southerly end of Moosehead Lake. Here we took a plane for an outlying camp. Our pilot-guide had a hotel-size shortening container in the luggage section, I noticed. He carried it into the log cabin with tender, loving care. Following a cocktail hour, he built a fire in an old wood stove and set the big metal can on the hot covers. Shortly, water steamed around the cover and the aroma of boiling lobsters permeated the air. The odor to a seafood-lover's nostrils is as delicious as that tantalizing smell of freshly ground coffee. We smacked our lips in anticipation. Served with melted butter and slices of lemon, the lobster meat was relished for its own delicate taste and, in the camp atmosphere, something was added which made the meal unforgettable.

We were off to a fine beginning.

Next morning, the pilot flew us to a long, narrow, shallow pond. He told us that, the previous fall, he had seen trout lying by the score in a thin channel of spring water a few yards off one side of the pond. It was the only "hole" deep enough to hold trout in warm weather, he felt certain. We launched a canoe and I paddled out to the spot he indicated. Then I pushed a canoe pole into the soft bottom and tied the canoe to it. I was seated in the center of the craft. The editor was in the bow; his publisher on a stern seat. I told them to cast dry flies. I would not fish, since we were one too many for safety.

As each of them dropped Brown and White Wulffs on the surface simultaneously, both were fast to trout. These were fish of about two pounds. They played them to my position and I released the trout one at a time.

Their flies were tied from unborn-calf hair, they told me. (I wish I had the address of that tier in New York from whom they had purchased those Wulffs. Size 8, they were large enough to be seen readily yet not so big as to make casts difficult. It was their flotation quality, though, that impressed me. They didn't dress them after playing a fish; simply wiped them in lamb's-wool pads and swished them in the air by false-casting a second or so before dropping them on the pond again for another certain strike.)

Yes, strikes were just as sure as breathing on that luckiest of days. All of the trout were approximately the same size and weight; all were deep, strong, healthy wild fish in striking coloration. I released so many that my fingers cracked open in places, as the trout thrashed and squirmed and pushed the fly-hook shanks against my wet hands. Only four of them took the dry flies so deep that I had to save them for lunch or see them float belly-up on the water.

Meanwhile the guide was ashore with a small fire going, awaiting our return. I counted sixty fish released before the sun laid its brightness precisely on the springhole and the action stopped cold. Those four trout were all we could eat, along with fried potatoes, mugs of steaming coffee and slices of homemade apple pie the pilot had produced in a magical manner from his big pack basket.

We loaded the aluminum canoe on a pontoon and the guide lashed it tightly. Then, we climbed aboard. He started the motor of the single-engine ship, taxied out and ran her down to the very end of the little waterway. Now, he speeded up until the prop was singing in a light breeze. As we sped down the liquid runway, the pilot rocked the plane sidewise until one float was mostly out of water. Then, the other pontoon shook loose of the watery grip and we climbed up on the step. The nose lifted. Air was under the wings. We barely cleared spruce treetops and the pilot curved her in a side-tilt around the pond, gaining altitude. Then he pointed her south and gave her her head for home base.

It requires experience and skill to land and take off on such wilderness waters. Planes have been lost and lives, too, on occasion. Hillsides crowd down to the water's edge in some of the more hazardous locations; winds must blow from the right quarter if takeoffs are to be achieved in the really tight little spots. Yet hundreds of trips are made without incident, when planes are guided by men who know the ropes as well as our pilot did on that occasion.

We looked back at the now tiny speck of water where the trout had hit dry flies so readily and knew we would always remember it as a magical destination. The publisher later decided we should not reveal its exact location or its actual name. "Let's call it Calabash. It's in the Allagash region, and that's near enough—right?"

That evening, after a swim in the lake fronting the cabin we had slept in the night before, we enjoyed cocktails and a dinner of prime steak, baked potatoes—even a salad—for the pilot-guide was a fine cook.

In the morning, we took fish from the dock, too, so they were fresh enough to ice for the editor and publisher to take back home.

They wished for weeks of this kind of sport but their responsibilities did not permit a long visit. (This, I decided, was fortunate in one way: Action of the kind we had experienced could only rarely be found when cold-water species were sought.)

Several years went by before the editor could schedule another trip to Maine; this time alone. We flew to a small lake that could be readily reached only by float plane. No roads then led to it. I had arranged accommodations at a fishing lodge. We found a dozen sportsmen registered there and were warned that trout fishing was slower than cold molasses running uphill in January.

It was spring—time to fish with bucktails and streamer flies rather than with dries. We went down the lake in a boat assigned to the two of us by the lodge proprietor, trying our luck along the way by casting in toward shore and retrieving the sunken streamers, then repeating casts. Nothing hit. I rowed over to the deeper water surrounding a small rocky island. Then I dropped an anchor.

"Sometimes, when it's this early and water is cold, we have to tease trout and salmon to hit," I told my companion. I made several casts in the same spot, placing a Black Ghost streamer near a cluster of big rocks, allowing it to settle to bottom and then bringing it back with sharp jerks on the line. After half a dozen casts of this kind, I felt a tug; I struck and was tied to a battling brook trout.

Now the editor bent on a Black Ghost of the same size as mine—a No. 6 on a long-shank hook. The streamers had yellow hackle wound around the throats and this sort of breathed in and out when the fly was in motion. I had been given half a dozen of them by the outdoor editor of another magazine, during a salmon trip when we had enjoyed fast action with landlocks. I was happy to share them now, of course.

"I use larger sizes of streamers in the spring than many trouters do," I told the editor. "I sometimes cast flies as large as No. 2; I use a size 4 frequently and a No. 6, like these, oftener than going to 8's and 10's. It seems to me that the fish can see the bigger streamers more quickly and, anyhow, the greedy—often heavier—trout strike the large patterns better."

Often, I explained, I caught brook trout while trolling for landlocked salmon in northern lakes in the spring of the year. This experience had indicated that a big fly was acceptable, if not preferable, to brookies as well as to salmon.

Actually, I do have favorites, like all fishermen: Gray Ghost for landlocks and Black Ghost for Eastern brook trout in the spring and fall. Dry flies in the warmer weather months, especially for trout.

Just then the visiting editor hooked a good trout. He played it well. I dipped it out with the boat net.

"This lake gets very little pressure, considering its size. We might as well keep a few trout for breakfast and to prove to the other guests that they'll take when the 'experts' go after them."

He joined me in laughing. How often we were on the spot to prove our capabilities and how often both of us failed to do any better than anybody else! So, this was too good to let go by.

"Maybe we won't catch any more . . ." I began, when my line tightened as a trout struck and I automatically hooked him.

Shortly, we both had fish on. "Guess we found a school of them," I said.

We kept four trout apiece. Trolling the streamers as I rowed us back to the lodge, my friend and I each caught a legal salmon but we returned these to the lake to grow bigger for later sport.

The guests at the camp were quick to ask what we had taken the trout on and I soon had given away all of my Black Ghosts.

"We're going into a distant trout pond tomorrow," I said

to the editor. "I understand we can catch them on anything there—so many fish and almost nobody fishes for them."

Anxious to prove what his area had to offer, our host got us up bright and early and after breakfast he and another guide ran us the length of the lake in outboard-equipped canoes. Then they paddled and poled us up a narrow, winding stream. The shores were so close one canoe had to follow behind the other.

Finally, we reached the source of the brook and took to a vaguely-blazed foot trail that led up ridges and down lowlands, through wet, swampy places and along the sides of hills one might have considered small mountains.

At springs here and there we stopped to drink the clear water and take breathers. I was toting several cameras and my fishing tackle. The editor was packing more gear than he might have if he had known how far we had to walk. The guides, used to hiking endlessly, were impatient to get to the backwoods trouting paradise.

Ultimately, we sighted water and after coursing the shoreline for what seemed hours but was actually only a half-hour, I suppose, we came to a log cabin and gladly dropped our packs and tackle on the porch.

Seeing our relief, the lodge owner said: "We'll be flying out. I asked a pilot to pick us up before dark."

This recharged our ambition and we rigged up and soon were fishing the shoreline water in keen anticipation. I paddled from the stern, my companion cast from the bow. Occasionally, we would drift so I could cast, as well.

When they called us to lunch we hadn't had a strike. Afterwards, with the guides paddling us, both had several hours of fishing. Not a trout took any offering.

I tried every kind of fly I could think of, most of which had proved irresistible at other times. The guides suggested their favorites. The editor drew from his vast store of patterns. We trolled and cast. We fished off the bottom, part-way down, on the top, just under the surface. The guides tried live baits.

When the plane arrived we went inside the cabin to pack

our gear. On the walls were mounted trout—big, husky fish—with the dates they had been caught at that pond. For all we might have proved, the mounted trout were the last remaining fish for miles around.

Once, in the summer that same year, I was flown to that hideaway and trout took dry flies nearly every cast.

That is fishing as one gets to know it in the making of an angler. It is the uncertainty that gives such excitement to those times when gamefishes respond in the manner they should for the "experts."

27

THE NEED FOR DECISIVENESS

and The Art of Avoiding Decisions

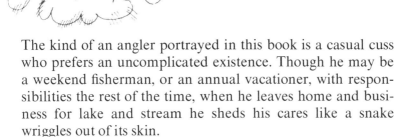

The kind of an angler portrayed in this book is a casual cuss who prefers an uncomplicated existence. Though he may be a weekend fisherman, or an annual vacationer, with responsibilities the rest of the time, when he leaves home and business for lake and stream he sheds his cares like a snake wriggles out of its skin.

He prefers not to make decisions in his off-duty hours, so he tries to think like a fish and select a fly, lure or piece of bait that should be attractive to him if he were equipped with fins, gills and scales, rather than with arms, legs, eyes and $500 worth of A&F tackle.

His chief source of irritation when angling results when finned quarry fail to appreciate the selection he has made to attract their interest. His aplomb falters when a fishing companion—who has decided that "They'll take something quite different from what you've chosen today"—catches a fish on his first offering, to prove how wrong you are and how right he is. "Just like I told you."

If the would-be casual angler wants to avoid such irritations, he has several minor decisions to make in advance and then, maybe, he won't have to feel his blood pressure rise, his competitive spirit come to the fore, or his calm be broken when bass don't bite.

Here are the alternatives:

(1) He can fish alone.

(2) He can imitate an old guide of my acquaintance who securely tied on a proven dry fly at the beginning of each season and—his leader stout and strong—cast only that one pattern from spring to fall for trout in the wild fish-holes of northern Maine. He argued that if the fish would strike anything, they would hit his fly. If they were not in a taking mood, changing to all the flies this side of hell wouldn't make a great difference. A season's tally doubtless proved his point. His big dry fly was *in the water* more hours than if he were taking precious minutes on evening hatches to replace it with numerous other patterns.

He believed that spinners, plugs, spoons and baits should be fished the same way. He'd advise an angler to choose one that has consistently taken salmon, lakers, or whatever the species sought, tie it on in the spring and, unless it breaks off, leave it there and keep on fishing, not changing.

This could be bad news for those who produce and sell those thousands of lures that catch anglers, if not fish. But, again, choosing one kind for each species and sticking with it can cut down decision-making if nothing else.

(3) A final alternative—He can match the fly, spoon, bait or plug of his companion precisely, on the assumption that, if fish hit for his friend, they certainly should show interest in the same offering from his casts and trolls.

This won't make an angler popular, of course. I'm reminded of the time I was assigned to take pictures of an established outdoor writer on a fishing trip. We were both guests of a transportation company, and a public-relations man drove us to the scenic locations I had suggested. At a few such spots, I worked several hours setting up pictures, to get them just right. My cameras were on tripods, so I failed to realize that the P.R. representative was standing behind me and snapping identical shots.

He was bright enough to duplicate only three or four of the pictures I produced and to know that these would be used to illustrate the writer's national magazine articles, above all others.

During most of the hours he was with us, he was well over the bay from booze and was barely sober enough to snap a shutter behind my back.

When our trip was over and the articles were subsequently published, he told his boss—who informed mine, of course— that he had taken all of the color transparencies used in the magazines. And he had saved the single pictures he had taken behind me as proof that they were duplicates of those *he* had given to the writer.

Even though I requested and received a letter from the free-lance writer, stating that *I*, not the P.R. man, had worked hard, stayed sober and given him all of the transparencies subsequently published, neither his boss nor mine believed me and the writer, so far as I could ascertain afterwards.

So, alternative number 3 isn't personally recommended. Not unless you want to get a companion's fly in your ear or his plug in your posterior. Accidents can happen to anglers of low repute, though there are not many in this category, thank the Lord.

In making casual decisions, then, it is only to wonder "If" (I do this or that) what will be the effect on my fishing.

Kipling answered how to pick the right decisions in the making of a man, when he wrote his poem "If." Yet the anglers I know—including myself—fall short of his ideal image. I am more attuned to the simple answers to a supposition. For instance, *if* my aunt had testes she would be my uncle.

If an eagle swallowed a live frog and flew high above the earth and *if* the frog were digested to a point that the frog could look out of the eagle's anus and *if* the frog could talk eagle language and *if* he asked:

"Mr. Eagle, how high up are we?" And *if* the eagle could talk back to the frog and tell him, "Five thousand feet," and *if* the frog were astounded as well as frightened, and *if* he quavered, "You wouldn't be crapping me, would you, Mr. Eagle?" why, then, it seems to me that it would be up to the eagle to make a quick decision and that the problem would be taken out of the frog's legs. (Frogs don't have hands, so I can't see how the problem could be taken from any appendage except his legs, do you?)

If wishes were horses beggars could ride, as an old saying goes. *If* myths were believed then Pegasus had wings and *if* he were friendly toward frogs then he might have become a high horse and rescued the frantic frog from a fate worse than falling.

Once I was way out-fished by a friend. *If* I had not been overconfident by thinking I had all the sizes and patterns of flies I would need to take brook trout and perhaps a land-locked salmon or two from Caucomagomac Stream in northern Maine, then I might have enjoyed similar action to his for another kind of fish entirely—whitefish.

We were on the river in June, wading slowly and casting for an occasional brookie and a rarer landlock. Then, my companion hooked a scrappy battler from a swift run of water against the far bank. He had seen rises there and had studied a hatch of tiny flies when the rising fish had ignored larger dries. He had then tied on a No. 18. Immediately, as he dropped this on the fast slick, he was into a strong antagonist. We both thought it to be a landlocked salmon.

It fought hard but he worked it out of the run, across a pool, through a short rapids and to his net. As he lifted it, we both exclaimed, "Whitefish!"

I hadn't caught many of this species—a few in the northern lakes but none in outlet rivers like the one we were fishing. We were staying in a camp a few miles across Caucomagomac Lake. I had brought to the stream three boxes of flies, all intended for less selective fish than these whitefish turned out to be. They were as fussy as brown trout.

My friend had the little fly they wanted. I did not. I moved upstream where other whitefish were rising. I tried several patterns and sizes and when I chose a No. 16 Cooper's Bug dry, I had follow-ups but no hits.

I called to my companion: "What, exactly, are you using?"

He was now playing his fourth or fifth whitefish and was shouting with glee at the antics and strength of each one he caught.

"I've got on an 18 No-Hackle Dun. They love it!"

An excellent, skillful flytier, he had studied Doug Swisher's and Carl Richard's written description of this unique pattern and had promptly added half a dozen to his big book of patterns.

I didn't want to bother him while he was having such fine action and, anyhow, I was just stubborn enough to think I could fool those selective whitefish with something similar. So, I changed the Cooper's Bug for a small dun winged hackle and clipped the hackle off the fly. I hooked a whitefish on my second cast, played it nearly to net, stooped to scoop it up when it made another short run and broke my leader.

By this time it was growing dusky and I was fighting swarms of vicious black flies. I finally tied on another tippet, picked out another No. 16 fly, trimmed off the hackle and made a cast or two. It didn't ride well in the water. My patience was giving out. I lifted my shirttail and saw that there was a wide band of fly bites around my belly. That did it. I called to my friend, "I'm going up to the lake shore. Maybe there'll be more wind. Flies are chewing me alive."

When he joined me it was full dark. He had a nice string of whitefish—a choice foodfish—to take back to camp. He was enthusiastic about the fighting quality and selective feeding habits of this species. We promised each other that we would return to the stream again the next time we were in that section of the state.

Did I decide that this experience negated the advice and practice of the old guide, who bent on one big dry floater in the spring and fished it to season's end? Not when he sought brook trout and salmon, perhaps, but certainly if he wanted to take whitefish. I knew, too, that my decision when fishing for brown trout would have to be to match the hatch or fail to interest many brownies.

Thus, I admit, there are small decisions to be made by a developing angler. Not trying problems to decide but minor judgments about when, where and especially how to fish. It is still an "iffy" pastime.

28

TWENTIETH QUALIFICATION:

Deduction

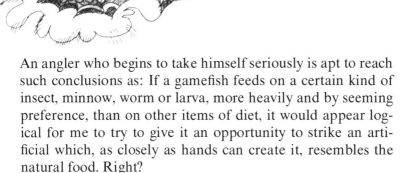

An angler who begins to take himself seriously is apt to reach such conclusions as: If a gamefish feeds on a certain kind of insect, minnow, worm or larva, more heavily and by seeming preference, than on other items of diet, it would appear logical for me to try to give it an opportunity to strike an artificial which, as closely as hands can create it, resembles the natural food. Right?

(The question may be directed to his inner self and not to a fishing acquaintance, until and unless he has had a chance to prove such a deduction beforehand.)

It's like a farmer figuring that if he breeds a purebred bull to a registered cow, which has set records for milk production, then any heifers born of this union will also be quantity milk producers. And they should be, unless a gene here and there gets misplaced; in which case a calf may be ill-formed and bear a name like one a farmer-friend of mine called "Screw-Bill."

Or, in the case of humans born of industrious, well-off parentage, the progeny may turn out as useless, wasteful piscators who, in the words of one irate ancestor, apparently lived only to "Piss their inheritance against a stone wall."

I have indicated earlier in this persiflage that I might fit into the above category—except that I was born in only moderate circumstances and have failed to increase my purse a hell of a lot.

Yet, to excuse my worthlessness, I turned to free-lance writing and photography that were chiefly concerned with fishing and related outdoor activities and, therefore, caused me to go fishing in order that I might have experiences to describe in outdoor magazines and books. It was one way of earning a living but it fell far short of the business-income rewards inherent in many other fields of endeavor.

It was necessary, too, to conceive new and preferably original ideas for articles and book chapters. Even if there are only a given number of ways to catch a fish.

Well, one hitherto unpublished anecdote concerns what seemed to be a logical deduction about the feeding habits of Maine togue—known in most states as lake trout. I was certain that if I could demonstrate a different way of catching them, any editor would get so excited he would call me on the phone and exclaim: "This is the best thing I've ever read! Give us more like it."

(What a dreamer! Who ever heard of an editor reacting to any manuscript in this way?)

Regardless, I had myself flown in to a remote fishing lodge on Maine's Chamberlain Lake—an eighteen-mile-long, clear-water, then little-fished paradise for trout and togue. Only one set of cabins was operated for sportsmen at Chamberlain, by a man and his wife who had become warm personal friends. It was early in the fishing season, so I was the first and only guest on that occasion.

My host allowed we could cross Chamberlain and reach a

lee shore for trolling, although waves were running so high they put the fear of God in my mind, that first day.

"It'll die down by afternoon and when we come back to camp, the lake will be like a millpond," he assured me.

To keep occupied during our crossing, I rigged two rods: a fly rod with sinking line and big Black Ghost Streamer on a six-pound-test leader for myself; and a stout trolling boat-rod, lead-core line, twenty-pound leader, swivels and end snap for lures, for my companion to hold. I didn't display what I intended to use on the second rig for togue fishing, since this was the original idea I had in mind.

He had a bucket of live smelts aboard, I noticed, but he had told me that the lake trout hadn't been taking for the three-week period since ice-out. I had deduced that my streamer fly, trolled just beneath the surface, should attract brook trout but that the togue would be nearer bottom. So I would photograph my buddy as he fished with the "idea" lures I had tucked away in a tackle box.

We reached the lee shore wet but alive and after bailing out the boat, my guide for the trip slowed the motor to trolling speed and I fastened my fly rod in a side holder and fed out line.

Then I lifted the lid of my metal box and came up with a saltwater striper-size jointed pikie minnow in green and yellow coloration. It was as long as some of the larger baitfish in Chamberlain, I well knew. I was ready for a snort of disbelief:

"What the hell is that thing?"

As it swung on the leader, it probably seemed as big as a cordwood stick to an inland-water fisherman. When I passed him the rod, where he sat in the stern steering, he exclaimed: "I'm not going to troll that rig!"

"Oh yes, you are! I'm going to tend my fly rod and shoot a few pictures."

It took a while but I finally talked him into dropping the giant offering into our slip-stream and he fed off the lead-core line gingerly.

The lure wasn't thirty feet behind the boat before a brook trout of about two pounds came up and smashed it solidly. My streamer fly was ignored.

I heard a remark: "I'll be damned! Trout's not much longer than the plug."

He pulled the brookie aboard and put the pikie-minnow over the stern again. This time he got the lure near bottom; the rod tip beat a rhythmic, pulsing sigh in the cold spring air and I could picture that jointed plug swaying and swishing enticingly through the lairs of lunker lakers, tempting them to smash it hard.

Sure enough, I saw my friend give the rod a boost and heard him mutter: "Got a good togue on. I *will* be damned! First fish so far this season—this and that trout."

After he had boated this one and then, shortly, had hooked a second lake trout and was playing it to net, I offered to troll with the rig he had scorned.

"Try and take it away from me! Just stick with your cameras. And, by the way, how about catching a fish on a fly?"

I told him to go to hell but he knew I was laughing inside.

When we were one fish short of our limit, he motored into a little bay where dead trees stood bleaching in the weak sunshine. He suggested that I try casting here for brookies. Shortly, this paid off and he said, "Let's go back to camp. You probably want a drink, after all of *your* hard work."

That big saltwater plug and a couple of others of similar size were so attractive to Chamberlain lakers that we might have broken legal limit laws five ways for Sunday. We didn't. Neither of us had ever done so, nor wanted to, now.

I flew out in a day or two, well supplied with pictures and enthusiasm for my "different" tale of togue fishing. One magazine editor summed up things the way he saw them:

"Seems too unsportsmanlike to catch such noble fish as trout on lures of that kind."

I might have written back, explaining that, up in Maine waters, we didn't put our togue (lake trout) in the same category as *Salvelinus fontinalis,* which species I had written a book about and admired as much as he did.

However, I rarely have questioned an editor on the theme, style or reader-interest of an article. Each has his own rules and his own opinion of what he can publish. To me, a lake trout is close to a commercial fish (witness those caught this way in the Great Lakes when conditions were different than now). An Eastern brook trout is something else again—a taker of dry flies when evening hatches surface on stream or wilderness pond; a colorful, clean, strong combatant.

On a two-ounce rod a contest with native brookies leaves the outcome in question. I have tossed them a No. 18 Mosquito at Nesowadnehunk Lake in Piscataquis County, Maine, in late June sometimes and have had them rip off line as they skittered across the surface for yards, then dove deep, then came up again. Incredible action for those who think only of the hatchery-reared, hand-fed kind of brook trout, lazy and lethargic and no doubt lying in water too warm for them in the first place.

It does make a difference.

I deduce that I must have thoughtlessly included with my photos of the togue caught on the pikie-minnow a picture of that first brook trout my friend at Chamberlain Lake took incidentally. That would have done it, were I an editor myself.

29

TWENTY-FIRST QUALIFICATION:

Ingenuity

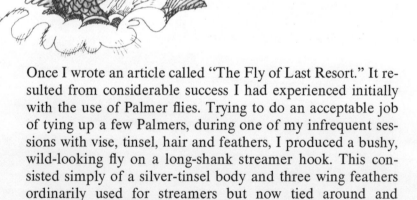

Once I wrote an article called "The Fly of Last Resort." It resulted from considerable success I had experienced initially with the use of Palmer flies. Trying to do an acceptable job of tying up a few Palmers, during one of my infrequent sessions with vise, tinsel, hair and feathers, I produced a bushy, wild-looking fly on a long-shank streamer hook. This consisted simply of a silver-tinsel body and three wing feathers ordinarily used for streamers but now tied around and around the shank like so much eye-to-tail hackle.

When dragged through the water, the feathers had a kind of breathing action and I later came up with a variation that included a pair of conventional wings, added streamer-style but riding over the feathery, long hackle—again tied to the shank from stem to stern.

Used for trolling at ice-out time for landlocked salmon, an

occasional surfacing togue, and infrequent brook trout, this "thing" (I won't call it a creation!) has been effective—more so, I think, than true streamer flies.

Before I wrote the magazine article, I tested the original tying (three streamer-wing flies, wrapped around and around the entire length of the shank) under actual fishing conditions.

I cast it for brookies in a western Maine river and took a few trout. Next, I dropped it on the bottom of a northern lake, left it there for five minutes or so, and, retrieving it, felt a lake trout of about five pounds tugging away at it. I was surprised that this togue sucked in the weird "thing."

That fall I was casting on a rainy, early-September day for big brook trout in the Fish River (again in northern Maine). I hooked and lost a fat brookie on a conventional Black Ghost streamer but I couldn't excite another trout to hit that pattern or a Gray Ghost. I could see them flash in the water but then turn away from my offerings.

Somewhat sheepishly, since I had a companion in the canoe, I drew out the "thing," tied it on a new four-pound-test tippet and dropped it over the side. After it had lain on or near bottom for a time, I moved it slowly, so the feathers would tremble. Then, I let it drop back and again pulled it slowly along to produce, what I hoped, was a breathing action—similar to a fish's gills, as it lies lazily in the water.

There was considerable grass in the spot I was fishing and the hook caught in the weeds now and then. Suddenly I felt a sharp tug but figured it must be those swaying water growths fouling the barb. Indeed, I said:

"Hooked on bottom." Then, "No! It's a big trout!"

It swam quickly toward the surface and we both gasped when we saw its size. This had to be one of the largest brookies I ever had caught in Maine.

The fish dove for its weedy lair and I soon was snarled up in good style. I tried to ease the fish and leader loose but, after five minutes or so, it broke and away went my chance of boating a trophy trout.

Notwithstanding, I brought out a spool of level leader material, this time in six-pound test, and replaced the "thing" with another, then cast it out and allowed it to sink near the spot where the big trout had struck. The coloration of both flies was the same: white feathers and only the silver tinsel for body wrapping.

It started to rain more steadily and we were about ready to quit when I felt another tug on the fly. Not a flashing strike, as is usual with smaller brookies, but a heavy, hauling sensation, as if the hook were imbedded in a drifting log.

This time the leader was strong enough to cut through the weed growth. Yet the battle was long and always in doubt. When I ultimately surfaced the fish and my friend netted it for me, we saw that it was a beautiful male, its markings sharply defined, its lower jaw hooked for digging spawning nests for females later that fall.

This was a trophy to talk about and I selfishly decided to keep it, particularly since it was a male.

I asked my companion to guess its weight and he told me, quickly, "Seven pounds."

I hung the trout on my scales. It weighed five pounds to the ounce.

A year or two later I was in the same area to try for another husky brook trout. None appeared to be in the hole I had fished before, so my same friend and I moved up from a wide section of the river to a narrow slick that fed into the pond-like part below.

A deep, fast, dark pool was the source of the little slick and I couldn't resist trying a cast or two there while my companion beached our canoe and the slick quieted down. Nothing happened until I made my first cast into the narrow run of water. Then I had a quick smash and was fast to a land-locked salmon.

My fly this time was blaze-orange and yellow, with silver-tinsel body. Hook size was No. 4. The orange streamer-wing feathers (saddle hackles) were wound about the entire shank of the hook, as in my original tie, but this time there were bright yellow wings atop the hackle.

The next strike was from a good-sized brook trout—nothing on the order of that five-pounder, by any means, but a fish of about two pounds. Then another landlocked salmon struck. Now another trout. Finally a third salmon. Five fish in not more than a dozen casts—and of the kind that usually are more reluctant takers, too.

I lost the fly on a sixth salmon—larger, of course, to our eyes, than any of the others. He leaped repeatedly and we could see that big streamer "thing" and a bit of leader stuck loosely to the landlock's cheek. He would sound and rub the hook free in the gravel in short order, we knew.

When I wrote the magazine piece about the Fly of Last Resort, I pictured scores of letters coming to me from readers who would want this pattern. I dreamed about putting a fly in a box on the cover of which was printed:

"If everything else fails, try this Fly of Last Resort. Fish it deep, while muttering, 'Strike this, you son-of-a-fish!' "

Soon, I imagined, I would be a millionaire from sales of the "thing."

Well, it didn't work out that way.

But I did accumulate a huge stock of barred-rock and red feathers and, if the moths hadn't chewed them, I might have turned to the production of feather pillows. Even of mattresses.

It happened this way:

There was a war on, and everybody who wasn't in the armed forces was planting a Victory Garden, acting as a blackout warden or wrapping bandages. I was living in New Hampshire then. My wife and I had four children to clothe and feed, so I worked on a daily newspaper and wrote free-lance material evenings and weekends. She played a church organ and taught piano. We did manage a sizable garden, mostly out of necessity but we thought and spoke of it as being patriotic.

In the church where my wife played, a new young minister arrived, along with his charming wife. They were North Carolinians. Remembering the southern hams, bacon, salt pork sausages and other by-products of hogs, he at once decided that he and I would go into the pig-raising business.

"There's plenty of room in the barn that goes with the manse," he reminded me. "We can build a pen in back of the barn and cut a doorway for the hogs to run in and out of."

Now, there wasn't any zoning in New Hampshire then but houses were close together, New England style, where a father gives his sons lots as they marry and continually decreases the size of his own and theirs, too. This was a residential community. The people were stuffy as hell, to put it bluntly. I could just picture raising pigs in that neighborhood, war or no war. Farmers kept them away out in the country. Never in town. Yet, used to seeing them in the South, the clergyman persisted that we should get ourselves some "hoags."

My wife's younger brother liked a joke as well as I did. When I suggested how we might lick this hog business, he thought I had a righteous idea. We picked up the minister and drove to a nearby farming community. One man had a piggery big enough to please anybody. We could smell it ten miles down the road. His neighbor had no livestock. He raised vegetables by the hundreds of acres. He was the kind of man who minded his own business and demanded that everybody else do the same. Tight-lipped except when angered, then he was outspoken, profane beyond belief. The oaths could roll off his tongue in a continuous stream. He was recognized for his profanity among some pretty capable swearing men.

I had chanced to learn before our pig-purchasing safari that his hog-farming neighbor's fences had broken down and that a couple hundred porkers were swarming over the vegetable-grower's gardens; they had done hundreds of dollars' worth of damage already.

So we drove the new minister not to the piggery but to the farmer next door. I introduced myself and my brother-in-law and was tersely reminded: "Know ye both—and no good of either of ye."

Unperturbed, I next introduced the minister—not by rank, not as a clergyman, but as *Mr.* So-and-So.

"He's in the market for a few hogs," I explained. "We heard you had some you wanted to get rid of."

After some ten minutes of the loudest, most colorful, explosive profanity I ever had listened to, bar none, I couldn't stand it any longer and turned back to get into the car. My brother-in-law joined me. Then the new minister climbed aboard.

We drove five miles in silence. Then the clergyman began to laugh. He slapped me on the knee and said:

"Guess that particular farmer don't care for hoags!"

Now, what about those hen feathers? Oh, yes.

I explained to the minister that if he thought the vegetable grower disliked pigs, he wouldn't have seen anything until our neighbors in town learned we were rearing hogs. He finally got the message.

"So," he said, "it will have to be chickens."

I didn't want any part of the hen business but I did feel a little guilty about our attempt at hog-buying, so I suggested another countryman who had large flocks of barred rocks and we stopped there to dicker. I pictured half a dozen of the day-old chicks and hoped that they would die soon. The minister went at it "whole-hog." He bought fifty for each of us on the spot.

We constructed a suitable pen back of the church manse and dumped them in. He fed them mornings and I checked in after work evenings, on my way to my Victory Garden. There wasn't any loss. I guessed he had said a prayer over those birds.

But there were complications. At the next meeting of the women's church group, his wife bragged about the minister's new venture to help the war effort. She was told in short order that one of the longest-time, hardest-working church members' husband was a poultryman, too. His breed was the New Hampshire Red. She couldn't see—just could not understand—how the minister could be so thoughtless as to buy day-old chicks from some profligate farmer who wasn't even a Christian, let alone a churchgoer in this parish!

That evening, we drove to another poultry farm, of course,

and purchased another fifty day-old chicks apiece. Within a month or so the two hundred birds were feathering out and the minister was suggesting that we crop off a few for our tables. I slowed him down until they had a little more weight.

Then he decided to enlist as a chaplain.

I had to find time to construct a henhouse in my tiny backyard and to move nearly two hundred chickens there.

Anybody who knows poultry realizes that hens have to have several square feet each in their living quarters. Otherwise they pick one another and practice cannibalism to an extent that can wipe out a whole flock.

About the time the pullets started to lay—and our kitchen, pantry and shelving were piled high with eggs—my kids would meet me on my return from the paper in the afternoon and cry gleefully, "Five more hens dying, Daddy!"

I would have to rush in and finish them off, then spend precious hours plucking feathers, drawing hens and thinking of oaths that became reminiscent of the vegetable farmer who was overrun with pigs.

One evening, as I stood inside the little henhouse, gathering handfuls of pecked victims, my wife called to me from the poultry-house steps: "Can you come out for a minute?"

"I'm busy!" I screamed. "Damn that minister, anyhow! If it wasn't for him I wouldn't be in this mess!"

As I kicked open the door, I saw her standing there with a stranger. She stammered, red of face:

"Bob, I want to introduce our new minister."

This was no soft-spoken Southerner with a sense of humor. He turned on his heel and left me wrapped up in barred rocks and New Hampshire reds.

But, like I say, if the moths hadn't eaten my feathers, I might have begun a wholesale fly-tying industry.

As it was, I recouped some losses and, with Yankee ingenuity, came up with a Fly of Last Resort, popularly called the "thing."

30

TWENTY-SECOND QUALIFICATION:

Reconciliation

It helps a great deal when an angler reaches that time in life which is sometimes called "Being Reconciled to His Lot."

During a trip to Bainbridge, Georgia, while I was writing this book, I fished for largemouth bass, bream and similar pond fishes with friends there. One typical February day I was taken to a small body of water in which dead trees stood starkly sun-bleached. There were small openings between the trees and, still-fishing from a boat, we were able to drop worm-baited hooks into these pockets.

The rods we used were a modern version of the old cane poles. They were telescoped and when the small-diameter sections were opened, the glass sticks were about eleven feet long. The fine lines were ingeniously rigged, so it was no trick at all to be fishing in a matter of seconds.

Our bait was kept alive in peanut shells and old leaves and

dirt. My companion on that particular occasion began to haul in fish at once and he continued to do so consistently. I wasn't as quick to hook and boat them and decided that, in the making of an angler, I had progressed too far in the direction of fly casting and had lost my touch for original, down-to-bottom worming.

The sun was warm and our day was highly enjoyable, nevertheless. I said, as I finally caught a bass, "Now, if I can hook another fish, I'll be able to tell the folks back home that I boated one now and then."

After a time, I did. So I decided "If I get one more, I can brag that I caught one once in a while."

This happened, too, so I was reconciled to my lot even though I didn't actually catch a lot of fish that day.

My kindly friends filleted a good mess of fish and packed them in a bag against crushed ice. They were as fresh as a daisy when I arrived back in Maine after a flight from Tallahassee, Florida, in the morning. My wife prepared a stuffing of Maine shrimp, Ritz crackers and a few drops of Worcestershire sauce. (Since the crackers were salty, she added no salt to the stuffing.) Then she rolled the fillets into shapes like crullers, with the shrimp stuffing inside, of course. The rolls were placed in a buttered pan and baked until the fish was flaky. (She warns that the stuffed fillets should not be overcooked.)

Served with white wine, the fish were delicious. As we were eating to our capacity, I complimented my wife on her skill and was reminded of a neighbor whom I had known when I was a small boy on a farm. She had a stock reply whenever anybody told her how delicious were her rolls, cakes and pies, and her husband and two sons would say in unison with her:

"Not quite so good as usual."

Reconciliation to living in the country then was a requirement if a person were not to become "woods-happy" from loneliness. Radio, television, automobiles—except for a rare one here and there—even telephones were scarce. TV's were unknown and radio still in the crystal-detector stage. We

used to get together and relate recent happenings in our localities, to dispel monotony.

There was the unlikely tale about a schoolteacher who, it was vowed with straight face, had one breast bitten off by a horse. Her grandfather, clever with tools, was said to have made one to replace it from a piece of soft pine. When she became pregnant, her father scrutinized the hands of all the young men in the area until he found a lad with splinters in his fingers. Then, out came the shotgun and marital satisfaction if not downright bliss. (What a blessing silicone has proved to be.)

There was a boy in the neighborhood who was not supposed to have all of his marbles. Once, while he was sleeping on a fishing boat with his father overnight, a dense fog rolled into the rivermouth where they were anchored. On the high tide the anchor dragged and they drifted into the ocean, well out of sight of land.

First on deck, the youth looked around in bewilderment. Then, shouting down the hold to his father, he cried:

"Pa! We're not here!"

"If we're not here, where are we?"

"I don't know but we're not here!" he repeated.

Some of the boy's neighbors learned a lesson when they tried to frighten this youth. Dressing themselves in sheets one moonlight night, they came rushing from a small cemetery as the lad walked an old dirt road beside it on his way home from makeup night classes.

Next day, he told this story.

"I saw a bunch of ghosts in the old cemetery last night."

"Ghosts?" a farmer asked.

"Yes, sir!"

"Did you run?"

"No. I had a revolver in my pocket and I yanked it out and fired in the air.

"Knew they warn't human!" he exclaimed. " 'Cause when I shot, they vanished quick as a flash!"

Years later, when I was living in New Hampshire, a story was told about two sports fishermen who, like the backward

Maine boy and his father, dragged anchor while asleep on their boat at night and awoke to find themselves in a dense fog. They started their motor and moved slowly and cautiously along for what seemed like hours, then days on end, though it actually was a comparatively short time. In a matter of an hour or so the fog lifted and they spotted a man standing on the shore of what later proved to be an island five miles from their home port.

The man, surprised to see them in such a small fishing boat and so early in the day, called out:

"Where are you from, boys?"

"Seabrook, U.S.A.," one of them answered.

Some years ago, a Downeaster, unmarried but with a roving eye and love often consummated, was said to have given away fresh saltwater fish to anybody bearing the same name as his own. Especially to young kids. A bashful youth, whom he failed to recognize, approached the fisherman on a typical giveaway day and informed him: "I'm a Jones. Can I have a fish, Mister?"

The Romeo rubbed his hands on his oilskin pants and studied the boy's features carefully. Then he sighed and muttered, "Could be! Could be, all right. Guess I've got a haddock left for this little bastard. Ayah. Never can tell."

Thus, others besides anglers have to become reconciled to their lot in life.

Once, fishing for cutthroat and rainbow trout in Idaho, I had to be satisfied with rainbows and brook trout. Just couldn't seem to catch a cutthroat on that occasion. My youthful guide didn't say much but in the afternoon he went fishing alone and returned with a full limit of husky cutthroats.

Again I was reminded that a resident sportsman is far more familiar with where to fish and how to catch the local species than a newcomer to the area can hope to be.

Yes, there are many ways and many places to catch many kinds of fish. One can try bait, plugs, spinners and flies in endless variety. One can fish deep or near the surface. One can troll, cast, still-fish. Fish can be caught in nets, driven into weirs, preyed on by otters, minks, bears and even by dogs trained by man to grab them in shallow water.

Notwithstanding, some of them are not taken by any of these methods. Despite everything done to baffle bass, bewilder bluegills, confuse crappies, enchant eels, fascinate flying fish, mislead mackerel, perplex perch, stupify salmon, titillate trout and wrong walleyes, these and other swimming species still have a lot going for them.

Man? Bumbling luck, meager skill, fulfillment of fantasies infrequently.

Then how does one get to be an angler? By keeping at it and—if he never does achieve what is a nebulous goal—by becoming reconciled to the fact that nature's creatures are propagating for his pleasure and as a challenge to his fishing ability and new trickery.

31

TWENTY-THIRD QUALIFICATION:

Adventuring

Excitement in angling may relate partially to the adventure of getting to far-away places, of finding fish abundant but people few, of facing wildernesses alone or only in the company of one or two companions.

Such adventuresome experiences were mine a quarter of a century ago in northern Maine. Today, seeking similar isolation, I must fly farther north into Canada, when the wild trout referred to in the following pages is my quarry. The pond once reached only by wings now is at the terminus of an all-terrain or Jeep road. Modern planes, too, experience little difficulty flying in and out, for their power and maneuverability take the "tightness" from the tiny trout holes once so hazardous to all but wild birds.

This, then, is how I described a typical adventure when, in 1949–1950, I wrote the following as a chapter in my book *The*

Eastern Brook Trout (which was later republished with the title *All About Trout* but is out of print in both editions).

DOWN WIND TO DESOLATION

The prop chopped the late July air noisily and heat simmered up from the wilderness as from a stove top millions of acres wide. At the plane controls, George looked as steady as one of his Nordic ancestors' clocks. The only ruffled thing about him was a thatch of weather-bleached hair. Under the circumstances, it was reassuring to have him for a pilot. The sculptor who cut his body out of granite gave him eyes with all the color and life of a backwoods pond when the sun is shining. Born and brought up in the Maine woods, he had been a trapper before the war; now he was back home, a flying warden perhaps thirty years old.

He twisted in his seat. "Nobody's fished this for two years. Last party to land here had trouble taking off. That's kept competition down. Trout have had a chance to grow. If you fellows can make 'em hit, you should have some fun."

He looked at me, questioningly. I didn't answer. Long ago I found out that it's unwise to predict the mood of a trout, but I thought, "We'll give 'em what we've got, George."

Gene, my fishing partner for the day, rubbed a slender forefinger over the well-trimmed, roan-colord mustache that hid a long, stubborn upper lip. A newspaperman of the old, hard school, murder assignments, the copy desk, city editorship and a score of similar tasks had forced him into a groove too few escape from; but he had beat the rap. At forty-five, he was outdoor editor of a chain of dailies with the state's seventeen million acres of forest in which to fish and hunt and write about.

His tone was merely conversational as he queried: "What happened to that other plane, George?"

"Cross wind," said George. "It sluices over the low ridges up here occasionally and sucks you back before you can get altitude. I think the pilot could have made it, but it's a tight spot anyhow, and with two passengers aboard, he didn't try— just sat where he was until another plane came in to help him out."

Gene nudged me, raised three fingers, suggesting that we, too, might experience trouble if a summer squall struck at departure time, planned for early evening.

We circled. Over the side I saw that the pond did look far too small. It was squeezed in the fist-like grip of the encompassing ridges. However, George banked nonchalantly. It is always treacherous to land in this utterly desolate wilderness and possibly disastrous to take off again. Grounded, a man would need a double-bitted axe in each hand and a hundred years of time to chop a trail back through thickets choked with fir and spruce and pockmarked with bogs hardly fit for a moose. Yet here, in northern Maine, is the last major stronghold in the nation of big, truly wild Eastern brook trout, long recognized as the game fish best regarded and most widely known by trouting purists.

In the torrid heat, climaxing weeks without rain, we knew we were too late for even tail-end spring fishing and probably too early for fall action. But you never could tell! It was our first opportunity, anyhow, for a crack at real wild squaretails in a busy year, so we had skimmed over isolated bushland the past hour in a northwesterly air lane from the seaplane base on Moosehead Lake, Greenville, Maine, to this tiny trout water, without a name on any map but known to trappers and pilots as Desolation Pond.

Landing, to George, was all in a day's work. Though Gene and I shut our eyes, we need not have been disturbed. He set her down as softly as a feather from the loon which shrieked annoyance and dived at our approach. We skidded down wind to a small cove where an ancient scow, left by lumbermen, lay partly washed ashore.

I jumped out on a pontoon but couldn't reach the skiff.

"Don't step off!" George warned. "You'd go under, head, heels and stomach."

I looked at the black, gooey bottom and shuddered.

Gene said, defensively, "Feel the water. Even in this heat, it's cold and clear as a bell unless you roil it."

Our plane had drifted off. George told Gene to stand with me on the one float while he eased in sideways by revving the motor. Gene clutched my arm.

"Stay back of the door! Don't forget that poor cuss who lost his hand. This would be a tough spot for a similar accident."

"What happened? When was that, Gene?"

"About a year ago. He slipped from the float, grabbed at the plane, and stuck his arm in the whirling prop."

"Okay, you birds," George called. "Get a line on the skiff and we'll take it in tow."

I jumped into the craft, actually little more than a long, narrow box, square on both ends, two boards wide and one board high. If we could maneuver it, we could stand up and cast without fear. It would never upset, that much seemed certain. I elected to ride in it, back to the lee of a larger cove, where George beached the plane and tied it securely. Here we found an old raft and a couple of spruce poles.

Gene shoved off on the raft. George improvised a paddle and told me to take the second pole aboard the skiff. Halfway across the small pond George said, "Drive that pole into the mud. We should be about over a spring-hole. I spotted two of them from the air. Other one's down the pond a ways. You can tell a spring-hole," he explained, "because the water is darker from up above."

I looked at George anxiously. "Think they'll be in the spring-holes yet? It's pretty early. Last year another fellow and I fished one of these wilderness ponds in September."

"How'd you do?"

"Frankly, George, we couldn't get 'em to hit until just before we came out in the evening. Trout half as long as your arm, too."

"They were in the spring-holes, then?"

"Yes, but this is six weeks earlier, and—"

"I've been thinking the hot spell might have driven them into cool water ahead of time," George said, mildly.

A few cumulus clouds were making and occasionally one of them would drift lazily across the sky to warm its back against the blazing sun, drawing shade along the pond for five minutes at a time. This happened just as I popped two clove hitches over the pole we had forced into the mud. Big trout started to rise all around the skiff. George said, "Guess they're in here."

That was an understatement, if I ever heard one!

My hands were trembling like a groom's when his best man tosses him the ring. I picked up my fly rod, stripped off line, and cast a red-and-white bucktail close to one of those doughnuts cut by the rapidly rising squaretails. The bucktail was dry and fluffy. To dunk it deep, I jerked on the line. A trout weighing about two pounds burst clear out of water, its body a dark shining crescent. Crystal globules sprayed from the fish as from a fountain. Then, like a diver jackknifed from a springboard, it flipped end-over-end and went under in another burst of bubbles, missing the fly by only an incalculable fraction of an inch. Thrills shot across my nerve tips like a charge of juice from a battery booster. My pulse went up a dozen beats to the second. I thought, "This is what I have lived for!" At the same minute I heard Gene shout from the raft:

"I've got one on! Wow! Look at that rod! What a trout!"

I was bucking trout fever when I whispered hoarsely to George:

"Big Eastern brookies don't come out of water that way once in a blue moon. We'll stick to streamers and go down where the lunkers are hiding. Could be a five-pounder in that school!"

As if in response, Gene called: "Mine hit a wet fly; number 14 Montreal."

Stubborn, hard to convince, I fished the bucktail while Gene played and released his first trout and a second hefty, scrapping squaretail. Their splashing antics and Gene's gleeful cries had me on the ropes. The trout around our skiff would lie in the sheltering bottom weeds for a while, then the surface would actually boil with them. It dawned on me, as if I'd been hit with a hammer, that they were coming up when the sun went behind a cloud for a minute or two. As it reappeared, ricocheting brilliant light rays off the pond, not a trout would rise.

"I wonder," I mused, "if this is to be one of those days

when Eastern brookies—the big ones—want dry flies in preference to anything else? There could be a hatch on that isn't
visible to my eyes."

George flicked a cigarette butt over the side. It drifted
back past my position in the stern. An enormous trout rose
and smacked it within six feet of the skiff. George had set up
my dry-fly rod and had tied on a big White Wulff. I grasped
the rod by its middle and without even waiting to cast,
merely dropped the fly on the water where the fish had surfaced. I didn't have time to work my hand down to the butt
before I saw the trout coming back, his mouth open like an
angry bass. Frantically, I tried to lift the rod and slide my
fingers onto the cork grip. It was too late. Instinctively, I
lowered the tip. That was all that saved the rod. There wasn't
any need to strike. When the fly snagged his lower lip, that
trout hit so hard he bounced and skittered on the surface like
a shot-smacked duck. Luckily for me, instead of diving under the skiff, he plunged obliquely away from it, burning
slack line through my protesting fingers. Then the reel began
to whine and I wondered if he'd get down to the backing
and, if so, whether it would hold.

Gene cried: "What have you got on—a whale?"

George shouted back: "Hard to tell from this angle just
who is playing who. Or, is it *whom*?"

"Get the net, George!" I implored.

"What! You're going to save him?" Gene queried loudly
and with mock incredulity.

"I'm going to have a picture of this fish, Gene."

"Besides, it's pretty near lunch time," George said, coming
to my aid.

Nevertheless, there was remorse in me when George hung
him on the scales. "Four pounds even," he murmured. "Nice
trout."

"Just one word to describe a fish like that, George. Beautiful. That's it, beautiful."

"Well," said George, "I'm all for going ashore and seeing
if he tastes as good as he looks."

Now that he mentioned it, the idea of food was attractive.

We picked up Gene, leaving his raft tied out for the afternoon fishing, and worked the skiff to shore. George took cooking utensils from the plane.

"Haven't been in here for several years," he said, thoughtfully, "but I seem to remember a spring about a hundred yards back in the bush."

He turned, leaving Gene and me to peel a few potatoes, dress the trout and build a small fire. Except for the mad screams of the solitary loon, the place was as still as a church. A whisper would have echoed off the ridges, it seemed. It was easy to see why conversation dies in the big woods. A couple of blowflies hovered over the fish and their wing beats sounded like a miniature buzz saw ripping through a pine knot. We could hear our hands swish, it appeared to me, as we brushed the flies away. Thus a crash in the brush stopped us cold in our tracks. "A moose, or a bear!"

But George reappeared, waving his arms over his head frantically. "Hornets! All around the spring!"

He splashed a bit of the water, as he put the pail down on a flat rock. We waved our hats and drove the insects away. The fire kept them back, as we gathered around it.

As the water boiled to cook the potatoes and for coffee, I thought how fortunate we were to be there. A slight breeze whispered across the pond. Suddenly it was cooler. The water, as blue as a woman's dyed silk dress, was ruffled now and the waves were white lace on frothy underthings.

Leaning back against the bole of a tree, I sighed in utter contentment. "This is paradise. Will it ever change? What do you fellows think? Will planes come here in large enough numbers to make a dent in the fishing?"

"We're pioneers," said Gene, simply. He rubbed his mustache. "This is Maine as it was at the turn of the century in the Rangeleys—Kennebago, Seven Ponds, Moosehead Lake—places that are still good but are familiar to many fishermen now. We're looking at the past and present, too. Incredible stuff! Those flimsy wings, that motor!" He stared at the plane.

"Yes," I answered. "Yes, Gene. But—that ship is a reality.

It represents something that may be bigger than even we realize. How big is it, from the standpoint of trout fishing in wilderness areas like this? To men like George, it's a means of patrolling more territory, of stocking more fish by air. But, *this is paradise only if left alone.*"

George turned the sizzling trout. His quiet features were intense. We were talking his language.

"If it blows much harder, we'll be here overnight. Just one direction to take her out, and I'd rather see it flat calm than to have much cross wind."

I nodded. Gene smiled thinly. Both of us knew what lay back of George's few words.

Gene was squatting over the fire, sniffing the trout hungrily. He appeared to be growing more solicitous about our lunch by the minute. He poured coffee, set the potatoes aside and held the frying pan in one hand, pounding the edge with a spoon. "Come and get it!" he cried.

We edged closer while he served deep, golden slices of trout that fell open, salmon-pink inside, and gave off such a delectable odor we drooled like hungry wolves. We ate the fish to its bare bones; then George produced one of his wife's pies from some mysterious inner corner of the plane. With second cups of coffee and that pie we wouldn't have changed places with the most fastidious of gourmets.

Finally, Gene cried: "Come on! Let's go fishing. Up here, remember, it's the first of June before it's warm enough to do much and it's apt to freeze up again darned early in the fall. It's a short season. Let's go!"

Nor were we long complying. George simply scrubbed the dishes with gravel, rinsed them and dumped water on the fire. Then we poled back to the spring-hole.

Gene agreed with me that big Wulff dry flies would take most trout now—the bigger and drier the flies the better. The wind had dropped again but the sky was cloudy. I tied on a Brown Wulff, No. 6. Gene's pattern was a Royal Wulff in similar size.

All around us, trout were coming up—fish that looked to be from two to four pounds. I was so excited my hands shook and some of my casts were sloppy and short. But it didn't matter that day. After a fly had floated on the surface for a minute or two, one would rise and smack it with all of the savagery of truly wild trout. I lost a few fish because my leader tippet was too light for such aggressive fish and I had to replace it with a stronger one.

"We could catch them on anything today, Gene," I cried.

Gene didn't answer. He released trout after trout; sliding his fingers down the leader, grasping the hook shank and twisting the barb free. This way, he didn't handle the fish at all and they swam off unhurt.

I tried to remove the hook from those I brought to the boat-side and soon acquired this useful trick.

We played and put back in the water trout after trout, any one of which would have provided the high spot in an average day's fishing. But the afternoon waned and we sensed that George was watching the weather.

"Any time you say, George. You're the pilot," I called out.

"Does look like a blow and from a mean quarter," he told us.

So we hurried ashore and tossed our gear into the plane. Even then, wind sluiced over the ridges, rocking the spruces until they wailed in agony. The sky put on mourning. Lightning ripped jagged seams in the fabric of the heavens. Thunder rumbled and echoed in the belly of the wilderness. Now, it cannonaded from one mountainside to another in a crescendo, until the earth shook with its fury. Before George spoke, we knew we were too late to leave.

There was an ancient, log-rotting trapper's cabin back from the shore. George checked the lines holding the plane. Then we ran for the meager shelter of the old camp. Rain dripped through the sprung cedar-splits roofing the cabin but it was a lot drier than out under the trees.

The storm abated in half an hour but George wasn't in any hurry to leave now. "Might run into another storm down the line," he told us. "We've a couple hours before full dark. Go out and catch a few trout for our supper and breakfast, in case we have to spend the night here. Keep four or five, to be sure, if they're two-pounders; less, if you get really big ones."

It wasn't so easy, this time. The rain had put the trout down and we finally had to resort to streamers, fished deep, before we caught enough for two meals—should we find leaving impracticable.

As we came ashore an hour or so later, the sun suddenly winked at us before it dropped behind a spruce-clad mountain. The sky was clearing, too. George decided we could make Greenville.

He unscrewed a cap on one of the plane pontoons and said: "Put the trout in there. They'll keep well. Too bad we kept any, but they won't go to waste, right?"

We nodded.

We pulled our safety belts a little tighter than usual, as George took her down the tiny pond and swung around at the very end. He idled briefly there, then gave her the gun and she rocketed through the water, her floats splitting double vees in the spume. George's face, I saw, had fallen into its old familiar pattern. There was about him a fatalistic calm.

He rocked first one, then the other float free and the little ship climbed onto the step. Now she cupped a vacuum for her nose but her tail dragged, as if she didn't want to pit her supple strength against the pull of the hills. The shoreline showed its teeth beyond. George yanked her nose higher and she shook free of the water all at once, lifting over the treetops but barely in a whining roar. More confident, now, she responded to George's touch and he banked her up in a wheeling, climbing spiral, like a young eagle trying its growing wings.

We breathed again and slacked off our belts a little. George lit a cigarette. I looked down at Desolation Pond and sighed as much with regret as with relief.

"We'll sleep in our beds tonight, Gene."

He grinned. "Lots drier than under the trees following a rainstorm," he said.

32

TWENTY-FOURTH QUALIFICATION:

Bartering

In the making of an angler, it may become practicable to exchange information on where and how to fish, bartering with others who have secret places and who know little tricks that take 'em; and to barter with brother sportsmen for tackle they have acquired to your envy in a swap of equipment you no longer value, perhaps. Such trading is traditional in all sections of the country and it gives zest to a fisherman's life that can only be compared to catching a wily "big one" which heretofore has evaded all offerings by you and every angler of your acquaintance.

It takes a particular type of individual to come out ahead in deals of this sly nature. Especially if an angler is to retain the friendship of those he tries to deceive. It amounts to the niceties of both participants either losing or winning equally. If you are generous to a fault, your magnanimity may be

197

misunderstood for stupidity. As my English mother once re-marked when my Scots father exhausted her patience by giv-ing a drunk a dollar to sober up on:

"They say the Scotch are shrewd and tight-fisted, but your father would give away his ass and excrete through his ribs!"

She used to hate the sight, smell and evidence of alcohol to a degree that marked many women of her generation—a time when social imbibing was rare and when males, like bad boys, drank to get drunk and show who was boss in their own houses. As money changed hands, from my father's to some poor inebriate, she would tell him:

"I wouldn't give such a worthless individual a thin dime, let alone a dollar! I'd see his tongue run out a yard and still not pander his prostitution of prohibition!"

(The exaggeration of language was frequently used by the ladies of her generation, and husband and offspring were of-ten reminded that vulgarity and profanity were known to God; that "The Lord will not hold him guiltless who taketh His name in vain.")

So, driving to and from a country church on Sundays, I would change words to loftier expressions, for the amuse-ment of my brothers and sister and to my mother's vexation. As an example, when the old horse trotted by a steep hill-side, I would remark: "I'd surely hate to fall off that prec-i*pice*—or I should say preci*urine*?"

(All of which was practice for my subsequent bartering of words for editors' checks with which to buy fishing tackle. I know who came out ahead on such deals, too, but as Lincoln reminded us: "You can fool some of the people . . . .")

In actual exchange of items recently, nevertheless, I have a magnetized compass on my windshield that leaves me as be-wildered as a landsman in a double-end canoe, as to which is the bow and which the stern; it's an item I won by exchang-ing a reel with a broken gear for the compass.

Before leaving liquidity altogether, I am reminded of the time I exchanged personal pride for humiliation, in what might be known as a pee-pressing problem.

I was a guest of an aging farmer and his second, youngish wife. She was a schoolteacher and quite prim. I was spending the night before opening day of fishing with them, along with a nephew of the old man. Before we retired, I noticed that the bathroom was adjacent to the bedroom of our hosts and, as I had been shown to an attic room, I told myself that I wasn't about to come downstairs in the middle of the night to use the facilities, no matter what.

Notwithstanding, the old man engaged us in talk late into the evening, as we sat drinking beer together, and I climbed the stairs to my bed in the loft with some apprehension. Sure enough, between midnight and daybreak I awakened and felt a need to go. There was a chamber pot in a commode, I knew, since this was an old-time abode.

But, country boy that I was, bashful and proud, I didn't want to take that container downstairs in the morning any more than I wanted to descend the creaking stairs to the bathroom below. So, I did what we used to accuse farmer folks of doing, I climbed up on a chair and released a torrent out the window. Then I smugly climbed back to bed and slept until dawn—the sleep of the just and innocent—as I recounted it to fishing pals, subsequently.

When I was called to breakfast, I came confidently into the dining room, said "Good morning" to my friend and our hosts and remarked that I would join them again just as soon as I washed my face and hands.

The old man observed: "Didn't see you carrying a chamber pot when you came down."

I hesitated, flushing.

"No," he continued. "There's a tin roof over the window in our bedroom and we woke up in the night, thinking a hailstorm had struck for a minute or two, there! So we can understand you wouldn't be bringing a pot down with you. I hope this experience will cure you of bashfulness, son."

It did. I traded away my shyness on the spot, I might say.

We had a great day fishing. Caught white perch, a pickerel and even one or two trout, as I recall that day. I apologized for my gaucherie to the old man, as he rowed my friend and me around a small lake. He relented from the ribbing he had given me earlier and, to ease the situation, he said:

"I'm reminded of my own boyhood on another farm

where I was born. Some funny things happened to us then. One of our neighbors had a speech impediment and he passed this defect to a son. The boy and I used to play together, attend school and go to church.

"The facilities then, as you know, were very limited. We carried water from a well, cut our own wood, didn't have a flush inside; not much of anything except the bare walls and a roof over our heads.

"Well, one morning in a Sunday School class, the old-maid teacher asked my lisping buddy, 'What's the last thing your father does before going to bed at night?' Family prayers were customary in those times, evenings. But little Johnny stammered a more logical answer when he told the teacher, 'He pithes in the think.' "

People had fundamental religious beliefs when he was a boy, our host recalled. He told us:

"One of our neighbors wasn't too sure just what kind of convictions he possessed. He lived a moral life, helped his neighbors in time of trouble, took care of his own family, was kind to his livestock, painted his buildings now and then. But he raised the question of good deeds versus the 'Love-the-Lord-God-with-all-thy-soul-and-all-they-mind' business one day, when the woman minister—a strict fundamentalist—was conducting an adult class. She listened in dismay, then asked him, bluntly, 'Just what do you believe, Sir?'

" 'Don't exactly know, 'cept, Do to others as you'd want 'em to do to you.'

" 'Well! If that's *all* you believe, you're on the road to Hell!' she exclaimed.

" 'That so? Might as well get going, then,' he told her. Left the church and never went back."

Bartering? The exchange man has often made from the simple way of life in the country his forefathers knew for the more complicated philosophy of "Do unto others as they would do unto you—but do them first," and similar hard-headed bargaining, complicate the existence of modern anglers, if nothing worse. They take from the fun of fishing and destroy a man's rhythm in casting, unless he puts out of his mind completely the schemes and plots of business when he goes off into the boondocks.

Trading cynicism for simplicity may be impractical, but a person hardly can have it both ways. The poor man, as Bobby Burns once summed it up, has all things to hope for and to desire.

An angler has only a few requirements for happiness: the time to go fishing; warm friends in his party; a few trout, bass or whatever the species being sought to justify the trip. Lacking even these, a sense of humor and a feeling for the quiet places in exchange for the tenseness that comes from too much high living. A tree to pee against when his bladder is full of beer: a hidden tree he would gladly swap for an attic window high above a tin-roofed bedroom window occupied by an aging man and his prim young spouse.

33

ONE ANGLER'S INTENT, OR

Revelation of What Counts

In the final chapter of this book, I had decided to explain how I had become an angler—finally, once and for all, a fishing personality, possessed of erudition; not a countryman with a cane pole and a worm on a hook but a Somebody—a pulchritudinous piscator, if you will, a wise Waltonian, if not an ichthyologist at least an identifiable ideologist, whose flies and martinis were always extra-dry.

However, I was left in doubt by such hackneyed truisms as: If you're so magnificent how come you're not a millionaire? and, If perfection is your ultimate goal, what's kept you from getting going?

Maybe, I thought, I am a mime, a fishing fool, a bass-busting buffoon, a theatrical trouter, a swordfish swallower, an eel-eating, elfish, embryonic empiricist. If even that.

Then it occurred to me that I was something in between—an average angler, after all.

This was a letdown, a put-down and a downer. Yet, I came to realize that if I had indeed reached the top then I would have nothing left to fish for; that my lot would be cast with those few perfectionists in our pastime, whom (to the everyday angler, at least) nothing so greatly resembles the east-end-of-a-horse-going-west.

This is meant to be a book for fun, not a treatise. I have every morning on awakening at my time in life but two things in mind, one of which is to go fishing. (The other item shrinks by comparison.)

To show how highly I place fishing, I had a prostatitis corrected over the Christmas holidays, so I would be in shape to start the spring fishing season. Yes, I took Tiny Tim into surgery well before the ice went out that year. I've had a dry fly ever since.

There are so many sources on what tackle to use, where to go, when to fish for each species of gamefish, how to build rods, tie flies, assemble leaders and tie knots the Boy Scouts never heard of, that my readers and I need never be in doubt about the essentials of angling information. Like many other sportsmen, I have absorbed so much of it that I drip angling adages like a sponge.

What, then, does this book teach a reader about angling? If, as many intelligent people believe nowadays, every written text should instruct as well as entertain, *The Making of an Angler* is a dud. The message meant is something like this:

When we go fishing we leave behind telephones, television, talkathons and tintinnabulation. We inherit quietude, inactivity, serenity, tranquillity, peace of mind and a passion for piscatorial pursuits as all-important, justifiable at the moment and satisfying to our psyches—for fishing is a primitive urge to provide proteins for our progeny, as well as being just a hell of a lot of pure fun.

If our fishing trips are with congenial companions, we

probably have a few cocktails in the evenings and, as our inhibitions subside, we relate what seem to us at the moment,
at least, a few hoary, humorous incidents about other angling
expeditions. Sooner than later, somebody brings up sex and
those who have enjoyed the mildest experiences in this area
tell the wildest tales, implying personal prowess perhaps.

When anybody in the crowd actually catches a fish that is
something to brag about, indeed.

Thus, this book's contents might be interpreted as factual,
not fallacious—with the exception of phallic fantasies, concerning which just everybody is a damned liar, so far as the
author can determine. Talk about fishing lies!

Anyhow, the intention has been not to play down worming, bobbing for eels, bottom-dragging "hardware" for lake
trout, trolling a Christmas-Tree for stripers. (If you don't
know what kind of a gimmicky lure this contraption is, check
the saltwater bass boys off Cuttyhunk, Mass.) Nor has the
thought been to immortalize dry-fly fishing for salmon and
trout—although, in fairness, some prejudices have been written here about this kind of ethical angling, so-called.

Live and let live—gamefishes and all, if this is your bag.
Otherwise, fry the fillets, bake the bodies and do your own
thing, in your own personal way. For an angler worth his salt
or smoke house is above criticism of his compatriots.

With this revelation of intent stated somewhat less than
succinctly above, it's time to go fishing, once more. This
time, for a mixed bag.

My home for a few days was a Dynavan camper—a
Chevvy van converted into a truck camper by a Maine firm.
My destination was a campground near the Maine-New
Brunswick boundary. The time was early June. I arrived at
midday.

When I inquired about the prospect for catching a few
fish, I was told that "They're taking a few landlocked salmon
in Grand Lake Stream." (This is a connecting waterway between what Mainers know as West Grand Lake and Big
Lake in Washington County. It is a short, wadable river in
most sections but with a falls below a fairly deep pool.)

I drove there in a hurry, of course.

Donning waders and rigging a fly rod, I tied on a Gray Ghost streamer, one of the popular salmon flies in Maine. I started fishing at the deep pool. There was a lot of water in the stream that day, so I had to cast from a small gravel bar. As the Gray Ghost sank from the weight of my sinking line, I twitched the rod to straighten my leader.

There was a smashing strike. Only a fresh-run Atlantic salmon from the sea can match in ferocity its landlocked relative. My quarry leaped, slammed down across the leader, sounded and surfaced repeatedly. Its frequent airborne jumps were like the takeoffs of a miniature helicopter.

I gave line grudgingly; retrieved some finally. I moved downriver as the salmon attained a current at the tail of the pool. For its length and immaturity, that fish was a devil, if ever I had played one.

Ultimately I got below him and worked in line cautiously until he lay near enough to net. This one—maybe the only fish I would catch here today—was a keeper for photographing and for my dinner that evening.

Once a gamefish takes a fly so quickly, I continue to use the same pattern. Superstition? Perhaps. However, I believe a hooked fish leaves its scent on a fly and this odor will attract others more readily than will a human-handled fresh offering.

This time, I needed more than conviction, nevertheless. I cast the fast rips below the falls until the sun set. No soap. A light wind died. The sky in the west was glorious. Evening birds were melodious. Frogs croaked bass notes. I breathed deeply of the fragrant air, moist from the river and rich with the smell of evergreens. When light mist lay over the stream, I turned toward my vehicle and drove slowly back to my campsite.

In the morning, I was anxious to find out if the small-mouth bass were on their spawning beds and hence savage, madly protective of their nests, ready to smash at a streamer fly or popper. I had engaged a guide for the day and soon met him at one of his favorite bass lakes. Boarding his twenty-foot canoe, I took a bow seat. He started his outboard motor and steered me slowly along the shoreline so I could make casts in toward the land and draw my offerings back toward the canoe.

I had a sharp strike before we had proceeded fifty yards. The smallmouth ran, taking line from a singing reel. I shouted, "He's a good one!"

Now the fish broke and spiraled into the air in a twisting, body-shaking manner that quickened my heartbeat by ten counts a minute, I was sure. As he somersaulted and dove into the pond, I cried, "Look at that!"

Like the landlocked salmon of the previous afternoon, this bronze battler brought credit to his ancestry and exhibited the stamina derived from ideal habitat.

Ultimately I brought the bass close enough for the guide to shake him free of my hook.

Now there was a fishless period. I cast various patterns, but none was effective. We had a chance to compare ideas and experiences about fishing in that area, the guide and I. One thing I mentioned was my belief that a fly for bass should be light in clear water and dark in murky, clouded, weed-grown sections of a pond. Looking over the side of the canoe, I saw that we were in just such an obscure part of the little lake at the moment, so I changed to a black bucktail that was tied on a long-shank hook, size 4. Casting this well out from the canoe, I allowed it to sink until my line went slack. Then I took in a few inches, so I could picture it as dangling half a foot or so above what might be a smallmouth spawning bed.

I jiggled my rod tip to bring the fly to life down there in the darkness. As it settled a second time, I lifted the rod rather sharply and lowered it again, teasing a fish—if fish there was in this spot. I could imagine the black hair swaying and "breathing," as I continued to wiggle the rod enticingly.

Wham! The solid hit by a gamefish, connecting a man's hands to a living, fighting thing, is an experience that makes a long trip worthwhile; that charges one's virility; that quickens the pulse; that takes from one's mind all else except this here-and-now excitement. When a fish is of sufficient size and strength to bend a bamboo rod into a quivering, shaking arc and to haul off line so quickly it burns through an angler's fingers, when the conclusion of a contest is always in doubt until the net-twine encloses the bass—then life is well worth living.

Boring deeply, running off in the dark water like a submarine, charging toward the canoe, still hidden, this one, it seemed at first, must be an overgrown pickerel. Then all hell broke loose, and a record-size smallmouth cascaded, after its startling ascension, so near our gunwale that water splashed all over me and I cried out in glee: "There's a real one!"

The guide urged, "Don't lose him!"

My hands were soft, now, as I eased up and played the bass gently. Would my leader hold? Was he hooked solidly enough or would he shake the barb free? Would I clear him when he ran under the canoe? Would he tangle my line in the motor?

Together, the guide and I, we teamed what experience each had acquired in many years of fishing. All that mattered was to subdue this smallmouth to a point where we might weigh and release him. Personal, family, state, national troubles were forgotten. Nothing else was of consequence except the outcome of this fish-versus-man engagement.

Did the fish play me—or I the fish—for five, ten, fifteen minutes? Who looks at his watch in the absorption of a contest of this nature? Certainly not a person who has dedicated himself to a lifetime of fishing, who has failed to become President despite his mother's early faith, who has accomplished little of a so-called "worthwhile" kind, who has still not been able to stand on his head and crap in his shirt pocket.

Was I thinking these thoughts instead of tending to the business of boating the biggest bass I ever hooked in Northern waters? What the hell sort of an angler was I to dream away my chance to be listed in a Record Book?

For that is what happened. The guide was swearing and

shouting at me. "Keep a taut line! Watch out, he's going under that sunken stump! Don't you see that rock with the sharp edge? If he makes that shelter, he'll saw off your leader!"

He even asked me if I wanted to hand him the rod and let him play the bass in the way such a lunker must be played, if we were to slip a set of scales under his lip.

I don't know what it was that possessed me that day. Perhaps I was thinking that if we brought the bass in and actually weighed him, he would fall short of the record size I already had accorded him in my mind.

Perhaps, in the making of an angler, it is the dream and not the actuality that counts so much, when the last river is waded, the final lake crossed. I wonder.

Anyhow, my admiration for that fighting smallmouth grew all out of proportion to the situation and I wished him his freedom more than I desired his capture. By far.

But he had to win it himself. Of what value is the unrestricted life of a bass—the shaking off of a man's social, political and economic chains—unless fish and fisherman are participants in a battle for freedom?

"You're going to lose him!" the guide warned.

"I hope so!" I decided, mentally.

With a strong tug on the line, I bucked the hook against the bass's final drive, and he broke off.

For a few minutes he lay on his side in the water, his gills moving in and out slowly. I motioned to the guide, who suddenly realized what I was up to, and he paddled me alongside the gasping gamefish. Gently, I slipped my hand under him and held the bass in a normal position for a moment. Then his fins began to sway. He squirmed in my hand. Now, he lashed his tail and put his head further under the surface.

The last we saw of him he was seeking his spawning bed again to guard the precious eggs laid by a female, we knew—guaranteeing the succession of his line, the assurance that there always would be others like him, if men and machines left him a reasonably secure environment.

I looked back at the guide.

"It's the strike and the contest that counts," I said, a little shamefaced now.

He told me, understanding: "That was a good one. It would have been quite a temptation to keep that bass. Don't recall ever seeing a bigger one, down this way, anyhow. The cold water keeps them from growing that heavy, ordinarily."

I cleared my throat.

"What say we work this shoreline the rest of the way to the end of the pond? You never know, there may be another one just as big along the way."

"If there is," he said, "I'll eat him skin, fins, head and all!"